Know Your Horse Inside Out

A clear, practical guide to understanding and improving posture and behaviour

Sarah Fisher

D&C

David and Charles

A DAVID & CHARLES BOOK
Copyright © David & Charles Limited 2006

David & Charles is an F+W Publications Inc. company
4700 East Galbraith Road
Cincinnati, OH 45236

First published in the UK in 2006

Text copyright © Sarah Fisher 2006
Photography copyright © David & Charles 2006 except: pages 6, 16, 20 (b), 22, 28
(tr), 36, 38 (tl), 39 (b), 54 (m), 55 (b), 56 (t l+r), 58 (mr), 64 (t), 65 (b), 68 (t), 70, 73
(t),140 (b) copyright © Sarah Fisher 2006;
page 96 copyright © Hilary Gibbins 2006
Illustrations copyright © David & Charles 2006

Sarah Fisher has asserted her right to be identified as author of this work in
accordance with the Copyright, Designs and Patents Act, 1988.

A catalogue record for this book is available from the British Library.

ISBN-13: 978-0-7153-2231-4 hardback
ISBN-10: 0-7153-2231-1 hardback

Printed in China by SNP Leefung
for David & Charles
Brunel House   Newton Abbot   Devon

Commissioning Editor Jane Trollope
Editor Jennifer Proverbs
Designer Charly Bailey
Production Controller Beverley Richardson
Project Editor Jo Weeks
Photography Bob Atkins
Illustrator Maggie Raynor

Visit our website at www.davidandcharles.co.uk

David & Charles books are available from all good bookshops; alternatively you
can contact our Orderline on 0870 9908222 or write to us at FREEPOST EX2 110,
D&C Direct, Newton Abbot, TQ12 4ZZ (no stamp required UK only); US customers
call 800-289-0963 and Canadian customers call 800-840-5220.

Contents

Foreword

Sarah Fisher has an uncanny ability to delve into the subtle depths of every horse that has the good fortune to come before her. Her intuition, compassion, energy and enthusiasm are boundless. This book helps riders and horse owners, be they novice or old masters, to understand how she does it.

TTeam, Peggy Cummings work and Karen Bush's influence on Sarah's methods are fully acknowledged, but Sarah brings her own teaching together in a simple and understandable way. Aggression, stable vices, long-standing problems and attitude issues are all explained from a horse's point of view. The rider, as an integral part of the equine-human bond, is also helped and encouraged to improve their own physical wellbeing.

This book is full of common sense. But sometimes someone has to point out the obvious before it becomes obvious to you. Sarah goes through exercises for the horse and also for the rider, independent of the horse, to help anyone reading the book to produce synergy – where the combined ability of both horse and rider become greater than the sum of their individual efforts. I applaud her.

If you have any doubt as to the efficacy or compassionate results gained using her methods, just take a minute to read her case studies. They are an inspiration for us all.

Nick Thompson BSc (Hons), BVMBS, VetMFHom, MRCVS

Improve Your Horse's Life

Over the past ten years I have had the great pleasure of working with some inspirational and empathetic people who have been pivotal in improving the lives of many horses around the world. Linda Tellington Jones, originator of the Tellington Touch Equine Awareness Method (TTEAM) training system (see box below), her sister Robyn Hood (also TTEAM), Peggy Cummings (Connected Riding, see box bottom of page) and Karen Bush (BHSIT and author of several equestrian publications) have all contributed hugely to my knowledge. I trained as a TTEAM practitioner in the USA and Canada, and the majority of the exercises in this book are largely based on TTEAM principles but the work of Peggy Cummings has to be included since, like TTEAM, it is a simple, safe and highly effective way of helping horses and riders reach their true potential. Both approaches pay particular attention to observations, respect the horse and use simple and effective bodywork, groundwork and ridden exercises that can be learnt by people of all levels.

Tellington Touch Equine Awareness Method (TTEAM)

TTEAM evolved from Linda Tellington Jones's classical background with horses. There are few people in the world with equestrian experience as diverse and accomplished as Linda's. She has won top-level competitions in a variety of disciplines including steeplechasing, Western and English pleasure riding and equitation, sidesaddle, dressage, driving, jumping, hunter, three-day eventing and endurance. Linda has been involved in the breeding and training of horses for many years and together with her first husband Wentworth Tellington, published *Physical Therapy for the Athletic Horse* in 1965. Her extraordinary career, spanning several decades, enables her to speak to and work effectively with riders of all disciplines all over the world. Her forward-thinking approach has contributed to the development of a technique that can help all horses and all riders in every sphere at any level.

In the mid-1970s, Linda started teaching clinics for the handling and retraining of problem horses throughout Germany. At the same time, her ongoing studies as a human Feldenkrais practitioner introduced radical insights into the dynamics of so-called 'problem horses'. In 1978, the formal system of TTEAM was born.

At its conception, TTEAM established an inextricable link between posture and behaviour. It is now used around the world by top-level Olympic riders, trainers, veterinarians, physiotherapists, rehabilitation personnel, pleasure riders and animal welfare officers. It can be used alone or in conjunction with other methods, and many trainers have adapted and incorporated some of the exercises into their own techniques. TTEAM uses bodywork, groundwork and riding exercises to improve performance and reduce unwanted behaviours without the need for using dominance, fear or force.

Connected Riding

Peggy Cummings developed her own system of bodywork, groundwork and ridden exercises based on 30 years equine experience. Like TTEAM, this system can help horses release old patterns of bracing and resistance. Her work has helped thousands of people loosen, re-educate and strengthen their horses and overcome patterns of tension in their own bodies that directly affect and inhibit the performance of their equine companions.

It's incredible how we can look at horses every day and sometimes not see the most obvious things about them. My TTEAM training and subsequent working life have taught me that the most important thing to remember is there is no such thing as the symmetrical horse. Horses, like humans have a stronger side, are uneven through their body and develop postural habits and traits at a very early age. The posture of the horse directly influences behaviour and performance, and many unwanted problems such as bucking, bolting, rearing, napping, biting and so on can be traced to specific patterns of uneven tension and blocked awareness in the body.

By learning how each part of his body directly affects performance and behaviour, you can take steps to improve every aspect of your horse's life, safely and effectively. You can make the impossible possible, the possible easy and the easy elegant. You can minimize the natural one-sidedness of your horse, help him to stay sound or recover from an injury and enable him to realize his full potential whatever your goal, while enjoying the benefits of a happy and harmonious relationship.

This book explains how to observe your horse to see if his posture is correct and whether he is happy and content in his work and day-to-day life. It tells you how you, the owner, can improve his physical and mental wellbeing. The experiences of a few of my clients are included to illustrate the link between posture, performance and behaviour and to show how with awareness and the use of the exercises described in Free Up Your Horse (pp.76–146), improvement can be easily brought about; each story is presented in two parts, the first in Assess Your Horse (pp.30–75) and the second in Free Up Your Horse. But first, here are two complete typical case histories that show the amazing potential of TTEAM and related appropriate therapies.

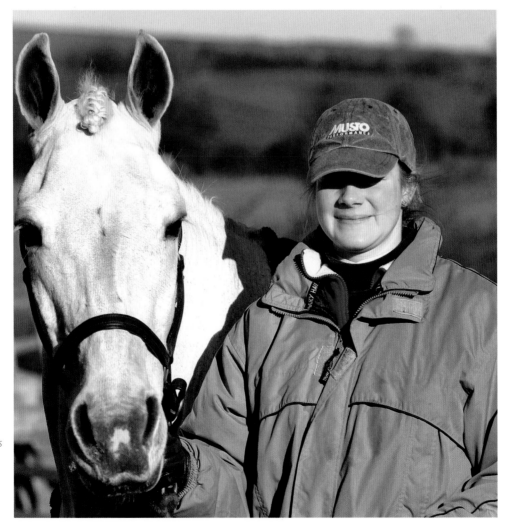

Corinne and Sage, whose story appears opposite

Sage and Polly

The stories of Sage and Polly are similar but their pattern is so common I wanted to include both to reiterate the importance of improving posture to enable the body to work more effectively, regardless of what seems to be the underlying problem. I often wonder how many horses have been written off – as Sage and Polly were or nearly were – that could still be in work if only someone made the appropriate changes to their posture and gave them appropriate care. Similarly, I also wonder if x-rays were taken of the feet of horses currently out competing, schooling and hacking quite happily, how many would show some level of bony changes within the hoof. I suspect the answer to both questions is 'a lot'.

Sage by Corinne Moore

I used to brush aside anecdotes of lame horses that were magically cured by 'alternative' and rather wacky miracle treatments; I was a happy and rather naive first-time owner who thought lame horses were other people's problems and lameness would never happen to me or mine. How wrong can you be? Two years later, it's me writing the anecdote – and I can assure you – not all alternative treatments are wild or wacky!

Sage is a 15-hand Connemara x TB mare. Prior to her lameness problems we were competing at local level in dressage, show jumping and cross-country to a maximum of 2ft 9in to 3ft. We were consistently achieving dressage marks of around 65 per cent at preliminary and novice level, and were successful in the local riding club. Then, in August 2001, 10 days before our first one-day event, my horsy world was shattered: Sage either overextended or was kicked on the suspensory ligament on her offside fore. She was box [stall] rested and over the course of six months systematically and under vet supervision, brought back into work. I thought we were over the worst, but early in April 2002, just two days after a lesson where she went really nicely, she became lame.

The lameness appeared bilateral, although worse on one side, and very concerned, I called the vet. Sage was x-rayed and nerve blocked by two vets at the vet hospital. The nerve block to the foot was positive. One vet diagnosed pedalosteitis (inflammation of the pedal bone); the other vet was noncommittal. My instructor and a few other knowledgeable people who knew Sage were rather sceptical, as her history did not predispose her to this diagnosis. However, I had nothing else to go on, so I followed the vet's instructions, which advised to let any bruising in the pedal bone subside. Eggbar shoes were fitted in front and I was told to gradually increase the work, being particularly careful on hard ground. I did this cautiously, and again she was working well. Then two months later while schooling, I let her stretch down, picked her up again, pushed into trot and she went very lame in front. My instinct told me that the problem was in the shoulder and that I'd inadvertently worked her too hard too soon and she'd pulled something. Within a week she was sound and I started working her again. At this point I decided to eliminate any other potential problems and causes, so I had her saddle and teeth checked by highly qualified and reputable professionals. I was told both were fine.

On 11 July 2002 I had a lesson with a top dressage instructor. I explained about the previous problems and so we didn't do too much, however, during the lesson, I let Sage stretch down, picked her up again, put her into trot – and just like before she was suddenly badly lame, and again I thought it was muscular and in front. Nearing desperation I called out a highly recommended physiotherapist who found a couple of things in her back and neck, but nothing that would have caused the lameness. She did, however, mention that she thought Sage's foot balance was not particularly good. Willing to try yet another avenue of investigation, I changed farrier and, under the agreement of the vet, Sage went back to traditional shoes, with special attention to balancing and increasing the weight-bearing surface.

I was still convinced that something in Sage's back and/or shoulder was causing the lameness, but having listened to the differing opinions of so many highly recommended experts and tried their solutions, to no avail, I had run out of options. Going on wasn't fair to Sage or me, so I decided to retire her from all competition and schooling and loan her to someone for hacking only. Sage is an all round easy to do horse; if she were human she'd be everyone's friend. I wanted her to be sound, but if I couldn't have that I wanted her to be happy, and she loves hacking. Before doing this, despite my inherent scepticism, I followed the advice of a friend and on 17 August 2003 – a year after the initial injury – took Sage to Tilley Farm to see TTEAM practitioner Sarah Fisher.

I was immediately taken aback by Sarah's intuitive, but straightforward approach. Not long ago I would have sneered at the word 'holistic', but that is precisely how Sarah looked at Sage. Rather than considering the problems in isolation – feet, back, tack – as everyone else had done, Sarah viewed Sage as one large 'machine' with many constituent parts. She picked up on areas where the machine wasn't working as it should, and explained the impact of one part on the workings of another. Sarah assessed Sage as being 'blocked off' in her back, thought she was not using her offside shoulder as freely as the nearside one, and said that her pelvis was crooked. She also remarked on muscle wastage in Sage's back that mirrored the contours of her saddle, which bridged and threw the rider's weight to the left. She recommended a visit by equine dental technician Lucinda Stockley as Sage's teeth had ramps and spurs and suggested I get her back checked by Leigh Miller a McTimoney chiropractor. She also advised the use of a wider saddle while concentrating on hill work to improve Sage's back muscles, and in-hand and bodywork TTEAM exercises.

My common sense side told me I was being led down the garden path and spending yet more money to be no better off. I'd already paid for the services of numerous people to check all these things, so how could this help? But, let's face it, if we listened to common sense would any of us have horses in the first place? Everything Sarah pointed out was visible and/or logical. Something just made me trust Sarah and go with it: Sage had the dental and McTimoney work done, I borrowed an extra wide saddle, which I used with many saddle pads, and we concentrated on hill work and walking in straight lines for six weeks. Things seemed to be going well, but I was terrified of increasing the work and having it all fall apart again. Therefore, on 6 October 2002, I sent her for two weeks' intensive rehabilitation at Tilley Farm. She was given a daily TTEAM session of bodywork and in-hand or ridden TTEAM and polework. Finally, she was fitted with a Balance saddle. In for a penny, in for a pound, I thought!

It is now April 2003. Sage is back in full work – just six months after her stay at Tilley Farm – and we started competing a month ago at local unaffiliated dressage. Not only is Sage sound, she is working better than ever before and is much more forward and positive in her work. She has gained so much muscle that none of her rugs fit anymore and I had to purchase new reins that were two inches longer! At competitions we come across people who haven't seen us for a while and they remark that she looks a totally different horse. Even dressage judges have commented that if they hadn't recognized me, they wouldn't believe it was possible to achieve such a dramatic change in a horse's way of going. I have video footage of dressage tests before these problems and after – the difference is staggering. We have been placed at every outing so far. It has been suggested I affiliate her and we even managed to pop over a 6in cross pole last week and still come away with four legs intact. Sage has never since had any indication of any pedalosteitis. Above all she is happy and sound. Long let it continue.

Polly by Sarah Fisher

I met Jo while I was working with a difficult mare on her friend's yard. When the session finished, she told me Polly's story. Having retired her old horse, Jo bought a beautiful cob, Polly, with a view to competing in showing classes. Jo went through all the appropriate vet checks before purchasing the mare and was understandably concerned when she went intermittently lame quite soon afterwards. After much investigative veterinarian work, Polly was diagnosed as having bony changes in the feet. Jo was devastated. She was advised to retire the mare, which she duly did. In telling me the story she stated several times that she could not bear the heartbreak of beginning a programme of rehabilitation only to have her hopes dashed. She loved Polly so much and, like Corinne with Sage, was considering re-homing the mare as a companion as she could not afford to support two retired horses and purchase a third.

When I saw Polly I was struck by the presence and the temperament of this beautiful horse. She was only seven years old and it seemed tragic that her potential was never going to be fulfilled. When observing horses moving I am always looking for the small details of where they are bracing as well as looking at the bigger picture. Polly's head carriage was unnaturally high and her bottom line was well developed with poor muscling over the top line. She had a slight tilt in her poll but the bracing that was going on through the base of the neck was so marked that there was little shoulder definition. Her back was as solid as a drum; there were little pockets in the thoracic area that could not move and where the soft tissue dipped away. Her stride was short, unlevel and choppy and she was blocked and rigid on the right side of her barrel.

I explained to Jo that we would simply start where we could and that in changing Polly's pattern of holding it might be that we would be continually taking two steps forward and one back. I showed Jo all the neck release work, back lifts and shoulder delineation and set a programme of exercises for the next two weeks until our next visit. We used the labyrinth, put Polly into Homing Pigeon, and showed Jo how to teach Polly to lower her head by doing TTouches on her poll and by stroking the lead line (all these exercises are explained later).

Jo is one of those dream clients – optimistic, realistic, sensitive to the horse and diligent about keeping up with the work. When we visited Polly for the second time, there was a noticeable and dramatic change in her posture. The bottom line was soft and almost floppy, the top line was beginning to develop, her back was flexible and, not surprisingly, she had vastly increased the range of movement in her shoulders and, therefore, her stride.

I worked with Polly over the course of the summer, slowly building on the exercises. She went from strength to strength and improved steadily and consistently. We put her into ridden work and Jo started hacking her quietly bareback. During our sessions we rode her with the TTEAM balance rein and in my wide fitting saddle. I also showed Jo some of Peggy Cumming's Connected Riding techniques (see p.5) to help keep Polly supple through the poll, neck, back and barrel. Every time we increased the work or the difficulty of the exercises I would want to hold my breath, but the short, choppy stride was a thing of the past. Even in canter the mare was free and forward going.

The last time I saw Polly everything was back on track. She had been shod again and Jo was investigating saddling possibilities. I didn't hear any more for several months and wondered what the outcome had been. Then, as I was putting the finishing touches to this book, I received the following email:

> Hi Sarah,
>
> Just to let you know Polly is doing fine and we have just started our showing. She has won three Championships and was second in her other class. Last week we went to our first affiliated show where she took the Reserve Championship. Polly is a dream to take and always behaves impeccably in the ring.
>
> I will never be able to thank you enough for giving Polly her life back. She loves going out and is enjoying everything she does. I myself have learned so much from you and I tell people about the good work that you do.
>
> All for now, and once again thank you.
>
> Jo and Polly

I am always amazed at what this work can do. And it wasn't me that changed the mare. Jo put in the hours and took on board everything I have had the good fortune to learn and can therefore share. Polly's story is just one reason that I do what I do. And, with a little knowledge, some patience and the desire to make a difference to a horse, you can do it too.

Body Talk

Understanding how posture relates to and influences behaviour in horses provides valuable information on how and why your horse reacts the way he does in certain situations. This knowledge is helpful when you are thinking of taking on a horse and have to rely on information given to you by the previous owner or when you are faced with problems managing a horse already in your care.

Making a start

Changing an undesirable posture to a more functional one not only relieves physical discomfort but also encourages more efficient body and brain use. A horse that is moving in a balanced way is less prone to injury and is more likely to stay healthy, as stress undermines the immune system. He learns faster, is easier to handle and train, and is generally more reliable in performance and behaviour. You can help your horse achieve freedom of movement by applying simple and proven body management techniques, which can be tailored to suit the horse and the routine of the horse and owner or carer.

Tension Patterns

Tension is not always unwanted. Tension and stress are necessary for all structures to maintain the ability to be supportive but they must be as evenly distributed as possible to prevent overloading in one or more areas. Specific areas of tightness and lack of awareness in a horse's body can be referred to as tension patterns since there are definite patterns of behaviour that are triggered by such areas. For example, a horse that rears will nearly always have tension around the poll and upper part of the neck. Tension patterns can be obvious and inhibit the natural movement of the animal to a greater or lesser degree, or they may be subtle and less easily detected, but all will have an effect on the way the horse functions on an emotional, mental and physical level.

Tension patterns can arise from birth trauma, poor training, inappropriate dental and hoof care, poor tack or rug fit, injury, disease, stress or inappropriate management. Conformation plays an important part and some horses are born with postural tendencies, also inherited from their parents, which can influence how they are handled and trained in their early years. Humans copy the posture and behaviour of those around them and it is likely that horses do as well, since visual learning is an important part of the development process for all mammals. Learnt posture and behaviour can exacerbate the tension that the horse carries from its earliest years and so the cycle continues.

Time spent addressing any issues, however insignificant they may seem, will create a horse that is more likely to stay sound and happy in his work. Because they influence how the horse thinks, feels and learns, tension patterns can hamper his ability to be trained, perform, accept contact, cope with the farrier, travel and adapt to new situations. When they are addressed, the horse becomes safer, more enjoyable to handle and ride, and utilizes his feed better because his metabolism becomes more efficient as stress levels are reduced or become non-existent. A horse cannot learn if he is scared, in pain or tense; it follows that the need for repetitive training is reduced in a horse that is comfortable. He will also become more consistent in his day-to-day performance, enabling trainers to assess more quickly whether he is suitable for a particular activity.

Punishing a horse for undesirable behaviour, forcing him to accept what you are doing or trying to push him through a physical problem makes existing tension patterns worse and leads to the creation of others; on the other hand, learning to identify tension patterns enables you to make positive steps to improve his wellbeing, as well as opening up deeper levels of mutual trust, awareness and understanding. At first you may not notice the patterns of tension through the body but as your awareness increases, your eye will become more sensitive and the more subtle postural traits will become increasingly clear. One thing is certain – you will never look at your horse in the same way again.

PHYSICAL AND BEHAVIOURAL PROBLEMS ARE RELATED

Behaviour and emotional and mental wellbeing are closely linked to a horse's physical state – and therefore his posture – and each can affect the other for better or worse. There is usually a reason for unwanted behaviour, and most horses labelled as 'difficult', 'moody', 'grumpy', 'sour', 'bargy' 'lazy', 'stubborn' or 'quirky' are in need of physical help. In the rare cases where a horse is extremely reactive and dangerous, veterinary examination often reveals serious underlying physical causes.

Understand the basics

This section provides some background on the nervous system, balance, proprioception, the horse's responses, sensory integration and pain memory. You do not need this information to work with your horse, but it will help you to understand why groundwork and bodywork are so effective in improving posture, performance and behaviour.

The nervous system

The nervous system detects changes in conditions both inside and outside the horse's body and responds to them accordingly. It works with the endocrine system but is faster in its reactions. It carries sensory input to processing centres in the brain and spinal cord, interprets the information and then transmits it to effector cells, such as the muscles, which respond to the signals.

NERVOUS SYSTEM
The nervous system is divided into two main parts: the central nervous system and the peripheral nervous system.

Central nervous system
- Consists of the brain and spinal cord.
- Receives input from the sense organs such as the ears, eyes and skin, and sends signals to the muscles and glands via the peripheral nervous system.

Peripheral nervous system
- Largely made up of nerves connecting the brain and spinal cord to the rest of the body.
- Undertakes complex tasks through a vast communicating network of nerves and ganglia.
- Has two important divisions: the autonomic nervous system and the somatic nervous system.

Somatic nervous system
- Controls the muscles for voluntary or conscious movement.

Autonomic nervous system
- Concerned with the unconscious regulation of internal body functioning.
- Consists of two sets of nerve cells that have opposite effects on the body: the parasympathetic system and the sympathetic system.

Parasympathetic nervous system
- Conserves energy in the body, decreasing heart and respiration rates, promoting relaxation, activating the digestive system and dilating blood vessels and so on.

Sympathetic nervous system
- Prepares the body for exertion, including flight, by tightening muscles, raising heart and respiration rates, slowing gut function, constricting blood vessels and so on.

The senses work together, and sensory experiences include touch, movement, sight, sound, pull of gravity, smell, taste and body awareness. The process by which the nervous system organizes and interprets sensory experiences is called sensory integration and it provides an important foundation for learning and behaviour. Studies in children with poor sensory integration show that they can lack self-awareness, self-control, focus and the ability to self-calm. They may also have difficulty in adapting to new situations, be clumsy, have poor socialization skills, and over- or under-react to containment, touch, movement, sight or sound. Many horses with behavioural difficulties or those that are slow learners display some if not all of these tendencies. Horses that are reactive when touched are likely to be more noise-sensitive and spooky than those that are happy to be handled all over their body. Touch is a versatile tool when working with any horse.

Balance and proprioception

Balance is a state of body equilibrium or stability where the horse is distributing his weight equally on all four feet and is able to move and alter his posture as required without the need for obvious re-organization of his body. Self-confidence and self-control influence, and are influenced by, self-carriage. Proprioception is the part of the horse's nervous system that tells him where his feet are without him having to look at them. It is also part of the horse's co-ordination system. Horses with poor proprioception and poor balance tend to be more reactive and more emotional than those that are evenly developed through the body. They may be perceived as being dominant, bargy or clumsy since their lack of body awareness can result in them stepping on or leaning on the handler. They may also be slow loaders or bad travellers since they lack the ability to adjust their balance as necessary.

Note how Harley has to organize his body to look right then left. He has poor self-balance and is tight through the neck, shoulders and back

The average horse at rest takes approximately 60 per cent of his body weight on his fore limbs with the centre of gravity being roughly underneath where the seat bones of a correctly positioned rider would be. The balance changes as the horse moves through the gaits and the centre of gravity moves back towards the hindquarters when the head rises. To engage the hindquarters, the horse must be able to distribute his weight effectively through his body. If there is incorrect muscle development, lack of awareness, or tension through the body, he will struggle to alter his balance through transitions and will have a tendency to work on the forehand.

The horse primarily uses his neck for balance but also relies on his eyes (visual balance) and inner ear (vestibular balance) for stability and position awareness. As the eyes and the ears can be affected by tension in the neck, muscle restriction around the cervical vertebrae will affect the horse's ability to establish true self-carriage.

Natural balance varies from horse to horse and is influenced by many factors including growth patterns, conformation, breed, teeth and foot care, muscle development, equipment, training and, of course, ridden work. The way we lead and handle our horses can have a dramatic effect on their balance; even though we strive to develop straightness and self-carriage in the ridden horse, we traditionally spend a large part of the time influencing the horse purely from the near side. It is probably no coincidence that the majority of horses are stiffer on the right rein.

Improving the balance and co-ordination of the horse does not have to take hours of rigorous training on the lunge or under saddle. Groundwork, bodywork and awareness are the keys. By releasing tension in the body, helping the horse to become less one-sided and by teaching him how to distribute his weight more evenly over his fore and hind limbs as required, you can enable your horse to develop the elevation and freedom of movement that every rider strives for.

TTEAM groundwork is a quick and effective way of improving balance and self-control

It encourages more efficient body use and develops suppleness and focus

Pain memory

Many injuries cause pain and affect movement; even after the injury has healed, the horse may still appear to be uncomfortable. This may be due to the fact that he has altered his way of moving and standing to compensate for the original injury and has developed an uneven posture, or it may be that he has an expectation, or memory, of pain.

Pain memory is a well-known phenomenon and has been researched in humans. Jay Yang, MD, PhD, of University of Rochester Medical Center says, 'We believe that the pain no longer originates with the tissue that was originally damaged, but that it actually begins in the central nervous system, in the spinal cord and the brain. The experience changes the nervous system.' For the horse this means that he may still be sensitive about having his leg handled or his saddle put on, even though the cause of pain has gone.

Pain memory can be frustrating and can cause confusion since it may be difficult to know whether or not the problem still exists. It is important to recognize that, whatever the cause, the concern is still very real for the horse. Bodywork and ground exercises can help to change learned responses by influencing the nervous system and improving sensory integration. Altering the pattern of handling, such as tacking up from the offside or touching the leg from the opposite side, may also help to change the horse's expectation. If pain memory is the issue, you should notice a difference in the horse's behaviour in a very short space of time.

Body language and responses

It is important to know how a horse communicates distress or concern. The more obvious language of the horse such as biting, kicking, squealing and pinning of ears is well known by every horse owner on the planet, but horses also have a more subtle language that they usually use first. By missing, or ignoring, early signals of concern, you inadvertently

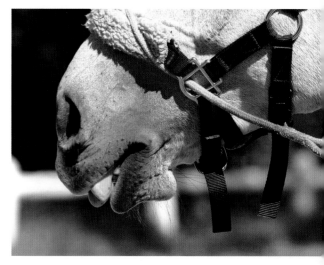

A tight chin and muzzle together with small rapid movements of the tongue are signs of stress

encourage your horse to express himself more loudly. Horses that use extreme language have often lost trust in their ability to communicate, and volatile responses can become as entrenched as the postural and other behavioural habits already mentioned. By shouting back or hitting a horse when he is trying to express himself we merely confirm to him that what we are doing is a cause for concern and so add to his stress.

When watching for signs, look for a pattern. Like dogs, cats and humans, horses have some means of expression that are the same whether they are relaxing or getting stressed. The way to differentiate between the two is to look at the speed and frequency with which the 'expression' is occurring, as well as considering the situation as a whole.

For example there are two possible interpretations of licking and chewing:

■ A sign of relaxation – slow licking and chewing movements and a visible release of tension through the neck and back.
■ A sign of increasing agitation – small, frequent mouth movements, accompanied by a tightening of muscles and shallow breathing. The horse may be anxious to move or may move quickly if already working in hand or under saddle

SIGNS OF CONCERN

Look for small movements as well as the more obvious. You will learn to recognize whether the horse is processing information or becoming concerned.

EYES – The eyes are often the first things to indicate concern or discomfort. Look for a hardening, widening or pinching of the eyes or a wrinkling of the eyelids.

The horse's eyes are a good indicator of how he feels, and small changes in the appearance of the eye preceed more obvious signs that the horse is unhappy

A closed or half-closed eye does not always mean the horse is relaxed

EARS AND MUZZLE – A tightening around the base of the ear and a tensing of the muscles around the muzzle often follow a change in eye expression. The set of the ear is another indicator of mood.

BREATH – The breath will become shallow or the horse may even seem as though he is holding his breath.

HEAD – The head may either lift or drop with the horse bracing through the neck and back.

SHUT DOWN – Some horses shut down, with the eye appearing dull and disinterested and occasionally a horse will shut his eyes completely although this can also be a sign that he is relaxed and falling asleep.

OTHER INDICATORS – Reluctance to move, rushing, frequent scratching, rubbing or chewing the same part of the body, digging, lip curling, turning the quarters, walking away, nodding, turning or shaking the head, lifting a leg, clamping or swishing the tail, and stamping a foot can be signs that the horse is unsure, uncomfortable or concerned.

Yawning can be both a sign of relaxation and concern

QUICK REFERENCE	
Concerned	**Relaxed**
Frequent shallow sighing and/or gulping	Slow sighing
Elevated heart rate	Calm, steady heart rate
Fast respiration	Deep regular breathing
Mouthing and/or grinding of teeth	Low relaxed neck
Clamped jaw	Relaxed muzzle and lip
Frequent yawning	Slow yawning
Fidgety restless behaviour	Stretching and releasing

The Five Fs

The horse has five reactions that will tell you he is struggling with a situation or alarmed. They will often be preceded by the more subtle signals (see p.17) but can also happen so quickly that the smaller changes go unnoticed.

Flight

This is generally the first instinctive response since it makes more sense to flee from a perceived threat than risk possible injury or even death through confrontation. The horse's head rises and his back drops. His senses become heightened. His heart rate increases and the blood supply to the extremities is inhibited to allow increased blood flow to the major muscle groups, heart and lungs to facilitate a speedy get away.

Fight

The flight/fight reflexes are closely linked. Fight usually kicks in when the option to flee is prevented. Real aggression in horses is rare and is usually the sign of a severe underlying problem, which should be investigated.

Freeze

This response usually occurs when the horse is frightened or unsure. He stands still, is rigid through his body, breathes quickly and shallowly and often widens his eye. A horse can freeze when he is concerned; for example, this might happen when a saddle is introduced for the first time, especially if corners were cut in the first part of his training. Freezing can be misinterpreted; for example, the horse is still because he is calm, or refusing to move because he is stubborn. Bucking, rushing, shooting backwards or rearing when asked to move all confirm that the horse was rooted because he was in freeze. If you see your horse go into freeze, stop what you are doing or are asking him to do. Go back a few steps to something he found easy or give him a break. This will help him grow in confidence and learn to trust you more.

'Faint'

When the nervous system is totally overloaded and when other options, such as flight, are removed, the horse may 'faint'. For example, if he is whipped and punished for not loading, he may lie down on the ramp or on the ground. This can also happen if a horse is forced into a high head carriage through the use of a gadget and then asked to go forward. Some trainers or owners assume the horse is simply having a tantrum and 'knows' that by lying down he won't have to do as he is being asked. In fact, lying down is an extreme response to high levels of stress and no horse should ever be put in this position. A horse may also buckle and lie down when approached by people if it is terrified of humans. It may also happen when the saddle is put on and, in this case is generally linked to fear, tension, pain, or an ill-fitting saddle.

Flight is generally the first instinctive response of a concerned horse

Fool around

The horse may mouth, grab the lead line, paw the ground, shake or toss his head, seem easily distracted, or fidget. Although more common in younger horses, older horses may also respond like this if they are finding a situation difficult. It can occur when working in hand or under saddle, when being mounted, tacked up, shod or trimmed and also when touched on certain parts of the body. Fool around can be misinterpreted as boredom or dominance but the behaviour usually changes the moment its trigger, for example the saddle, is removed from the equation.

(Above) Constant mouthing can be a sign of anxiety or discomfort

This type of behaviour is often misread as dominance or disobedience

Physical check-ups

If you are aware that your horse has a physical problem you must, of course, consult your veterinary surgeon straight away. While tension or discomfort in a large proportion of horses can be attributed to poor posture or ill-fitting equipment there may be underlying causes that should be ruled out. Depending on the diagnosis, it is likely that the exercises in the latter part of this book will help speed recovery, but this should be discussed with your vet.

One of the most important aspects of a physical check-up, and one of the most challenging, is ensuring that all equipment used on your horse is comfortable and correctly fitted. Reactive behaviour – however mild – when tacking or rugging up is a sure sign that the horse associates the equipment with discomfort. It is important to try to work out what is causing the problem and change the source of concern where possible. Be observant, listen to your horse and do not jump to conclusions. A well fitting bit, for example, may trigger a reaction in a horse that has discomfort in the mouth due to an oral imbalance.

Bridle and bit

If a horse has concerns about his bridle this will affect his willingness and ability to perform. An uncomfortable bridle will impede movement through the whole body. The conformation of the horse including his mouth, jaw bone, tongue and lips determines to a degree what type of bit he is most likely to find comfortable. Other factors that influence the feel of the bridle and bit are saddle fit and, of course, the rider's hands and posture.

The conformation of the head determines the size and fit of a bridle; some horses require a mix of the standard sizes. If off-the-shelf parts do not fit, ask your saddler to custom-make them. For example, a horse with a particularly broad forehead, as in some draught types or warmbloods, may need a wider fitting browband. The size and shape of the horse's ears will affect how comfortable the headstall is for him. There are now bridles on the market with cushioned and shaped headpieces that can really make a difference to the way the horse moves. If your horse is sensitive around the poll or has had ongoing neck or ridden problems, investing in a bridle such as the Elevator, which has the noseband strap running over the top of

The Elevator bridle spreads pressure from the head piece over a wider surface

the headpiece and not underneath, is very worthwhile. Designed by Lorraine Green of Horsesense Saddlery (see p.151), the concept of the Elevator is simple and logical. The pressure from the headpiece is spread over a wider surface area and away from the sensitive poll at the top of the horse's head.

Tight nosebands restrict movement through the entire body

Bit check

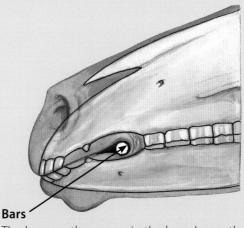

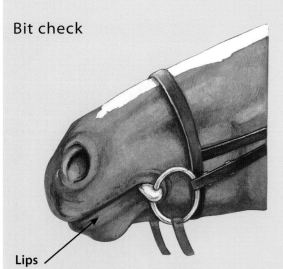

Lips

The shape and size of the lips play a large role in determining correct bit fit. Their thickness and length will influence how comfortable the bit is for the horse and may determine how the corners wrinkle when it is in place. As thin-skinned lips and longer lips will generally wrinkle more than tougher skinned lips and short lips, it is not possible to judge the appropriate height of the bit by the wrinkling of the corners alone. Instead of sticking to one rule be adaptable, use your judgement, check the placement of the bit inside the mouth, particularly in relation to the teeth, and above all listen to your horse.

Bars

The bars are the spaces in the horse's mouth between the front teeth and molars at the back. This is the place where the bit rests on the horse's gums. They can become injured, bruised or sensitive by rough bit handling or through the presence of wolf teeth including blind wolf teeth. Check your horse's bars by running your finger over the top and bottom surfaces. They should feel flat and smooth and not trigger a reaction when touched. If your horse has rough or sensitive bars, he is likely to react when bit contact is made, when the bridle is put on or when it is removed.

Tongue

The size of the tongue varies from horse to horse. Some horses have plenty of room for both tongue and bit when their mouth is closed, others do not. Drawing back the tongue, opening the mouth and poking the tongue out through the lips when bridled can be signs that the horse is struggling to accommodate the bit.

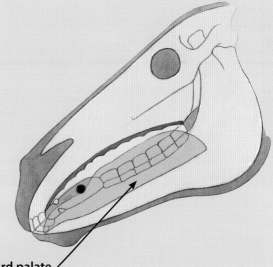

Hard palate

The hard palate is on the roof of the mouth. Some horses have a high palate and others a low palate, and this will determine how certain ported bits sit within the oral cavity. You can feel the hard palate by sliding your thumb carefully into the side of the mouth between the teeth and running it along the roof of the mouth.

Tight nosebands are not the key to a quiet mouth. They can cause tension through the whole body since they restrict movement of the tongue and jaw. A horse that is bridle lame or sets against the hand may have dental issues or other areas of tension around the mouth, head, poll and/or other parts of the body.

The bit is one of the primary means of communication between horse and rider, so it is important that it does not distract from what the rider is trying to achieve. A horse that is fussy in the mouth for any reason will not be able to learn or work to the best of his abilities. Tongue lolling, grinding the teeth, making rasping noises when asked for collection, crossing the jaw, drawing back the tongue or getting it over the bit can all be signs that the horse is uncomfortable.

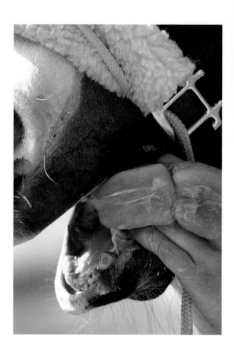

Tongue damage is not uncommon – this horse had an accident as a baby, but it has never affected his ridden work

Tongue lolling can be a sign of discomfort or anxiety

The bit also directly influences other parts of the horse's anatomy through its relationship with the tongue. The tongue lies between the bones of the lower and upper jaw. Some of the muscles from the tongue connect to a small set of bones in the throat called the hyoid bones. Small muscles connect these bones to the TMJ and to the poll. The TMJ is an important centre for nerves involved with balance and proprioception (see p.14). In addition, two major neck muscles originate from the hyoid bones; one attaches to the sternum and the other to the inside of the shoulder. As there is a direct connection from the tongue to the sternum and shoulder, uncomfortable bits and tight nosebands that reduce tongue movement can cause tension all the way down the neck to these areas. If tension exists through the sternum, the horse cannot raise his back. This pattern inhibits movement along the base of the neck and causes tension through the bottom line. As these are the very areas that need to lengthen and release for the horse to be able to engage and work in balance, incorrect bitting can be a major factor in poor performance and incorrect posture.

The tongue is a common source of discomfort. Some tongues are ulcerated because of sharp teeth and some have permanent damage from accidents or inappropriate handling, including thickening, lacerations, scarring and even partial severing. A damaged tongue does not always impede the performance of the horse but you need to study the tongue to make an informed decision about the type of bit best suited to your horse.

Bit wise

- There is more to correct fit and placement of the bit than simply looking at the wrinkles in the corner of the mouth.

- Look and feel inside and outside the mouth to check for areas of sensitivity that will be influenced by the bit: the corners of the mouth and lips, the tongue, the bars, the roof of the mouth, the curb groove, the nose and the poll.

Check for sensitive areas in and around the mouth

- Take into account the conformation and size of the mouth.

- Check the condition of all bits in use. This is of paramount importance. Make sure they have no sharp edges or worn areas. The smallest nick or raised area can cause extremely reactive behaviour. Make sure that no part of the bit can pinch the horse's mouth, tongue or lips.

- A horse that dislikes being handled around the mouth may have a degree of discomfort inside it. If your horse is unsure about having his mouth touched, use mouth exercises (p.90) to help him overcome his concerns.

- Check you are using a suitable bit by studying the horse's lips, bars and hard palate. For example, a horse with a large tongue and fleshy lips is likely to find a thick mouthpiece uncomfortable.

- Beware of cheap bits. It can be a false economy to buy a cheap imitation of an expensive bit – the balance and action may have been inadvertently changed in the cheaper version. For example, some cheaper makes of lozenge bits have one side shorter than the other, which make them unbalanced in the mouth.

- Explore different bitting options. Hiring a bit is an excellent way of trying different bits without laying out huge sums of money on anything unsuitable. You can ask for advice and be certain that you are making the right anything choices in terms of type and size when you do decide to commit to making a purchase.

Saddle

Saddle fitting is a confusing and emotive subject for many horse owners; it is also vitally important, as saddle damage is one of the primary causes of unwanted behaviour in horses (see 'Saddle wise' box). With many different saddles on the market it is hard to know which one is most suitable for your horse, and for you. It is worth spending time exploring the options available to minimize the risk of making a very expensive mistake.

Knowing what to look for in a saddle can help you find the best possible choice and will enable you to look for early signs that it is not fitting correctly. If your horse is overweight, has been out of work for some time or has suffered muscle loss through a previously ill-fitting saddle, it is worth working him in hand for a while until his posture improves. Once a horse is free to move through his shoulder, a hollow back will start to fill almost immediately: some horses change by several inches in diameter in a matter of months. When you are starting with a horse that has a poor posture, it is more cost effective to choose a

SADDLE WISE

Any or all of the following – and many more – can be caused by an ill-fitting saddle:

- Loss of muscle tone
- Dropped back
- High head carriage
- Sore back
- Sore shoulders
- Sore neck
- Bucking
- An inability to go forward from the leg
- Biting
- Kicking out against the rider's leg
- Difficulties with transitions and turns
- Problems with engagement
- Grinding teeth or lifting a leg when girthed
- Spooky behaviour or bolting
- Dropping one side of the pelvis in an attempt to minimize discomfort in the thoracic part of the spine
- Inability to stand still while being mounted

Raised hair behind the withers and loss of muscle tone are indicative of a poorly fitting saddle

saddle that can be altered, than to replace the saddle every few weeks. Investigate treeless saddles or those with adjustable trees, panels or padding systems that give flexibility to make changes as the posture improves.

Pressure from a poor fitting saddle can cause problems for both horse and rider

Changing the saddle and some simple exercises bring quick and dramatic changes for Nokia and Sarah

A well fitting saddle should not inhibit the horse's movement in any way or cause discomfort or pain. Bald patches, sensitive areas, raised areas, a scuffed coat, uneven hair or grease on the saddle pad or panels, blowing out the belly when girthed, reduced performance or reactive behaviour to the saddle being brought into the stable or being put on can be some of the early signs that the saddle may not be fitting as well as it should. Other factors that can influence how the saddle fits include dental abnormalities, fluctuating weight, an unbalanced rider or incorrect placement of the saddle on the horse's back.

SADDLE CHECK

While it is important to employ the help of a good saddle fitter, there are some basic checks you can do to see if your existing saddle is acceptable.

On the ground

- Stand your horse on level ground and ask someone to hold him and keep his head and neck as straight as possible.

- Place the saddle on his back slightly forward over the withers and slide it back until it stops at a natural resting place. It should sit well behind the shoulder allowing for approximately one hand's width between the back of the elbow and the girth. Sitting saddles too far forward is a common mistake and will alter the balance and fit of the saddle as well as inhibiting movement through the shoulder.

- Look at the saddle from the side (both sides). It should be balanced, with the seat level. If it slopes uphill or downhill, the rider will be seated incorrectly and will tip forward or back. This will cause back problems for both the person and the horse. The back of the saddle should not be past the last rib. A saddle that is too long will put pressure on the vulnerable loin area.

- Run your hand down the front of the panel between the saddle and your horse's back and feel for any uneven pressure under the tree points. The front panel must not pinch the withers or the back of the shoulders.

Use your hands as well as your eyes to check the fit of your horse's saddle

- While maintaining pressure on the top of the saddle, run your hand, palm up, under the entire panel along the back, feeling for even contact and a smooth surface. Check for any points of pressure or lack of panel contact. A lack of contact in the middle (from front to back) of the saddle, between the panels and the horse's back, is called bridging. If a saddle bridges there will usually be four points of pressure on the horse's back – two at the front of the saddle and two at the back. Pressure at the front of the saddle can contribute to spooking and rushing and pressure at the back of the saddle can trigger bucking.

- Pay attention to the stirrup bars. Some saddles fit adequately in terms of tree width but place pressure on the horse's back under the stirrup bars.

- Check that there is adequate clearance between the pommel and the top of the horse's withers. With your hand placed sideways between the pommel and the withers there should be enough room for three fingers in most cases.

- The channel or gullet of the saddle should also give adequate clearance over the spine and connective tissue. A channel that is too narrow, generally less than three fingers width, will impede the horse's movement and limit his ability to turn. It may cause raised bumps along either side of the spine. To check whether the gullet is wide enough for your horse, feel the width of his spine and connective tissue with your fingers. The channel of the saddle should completely clear this width, enabling the saddle to sit comfortably on the long back muscle without putting pressure on any part of the spine.

- Throughout the whole saddling process, listen to the horse. He is, after all, the one that has to wear the saddle. Watch for any changes in his eye or ear and be aware of more obvious signs that he is concerned as you tack him up and run through the checks.

In the saddle

- Ask someone to run through the same checks with you in the saddle.

- Once the horse is moving, check that the saddle doesn't move excessively. If the fit is incorrect, the saddle may move from side to side, forwards or back, or up and down.

- Be aware of how the horse responds once saddled. Does he stand quietly in a relaxed manner for you to mount or is he actually in freeze (p.18)? Does he move forwards, backwards or sideways? Does he stand waiting for you to give him an aid to move off or does he move forward the moment your foot is in the stirrup? Is his movement free and rhythmic or does it feel restricted and unlevel? Can he stretch and lengthen his body when asked or does he poke his nose or lift his head? Does he jig?

- Make a note of how you feel. Are you balanced or do you feel as though you are tipping slightly sideways, forward or back? Does the horse feel even beneath you or do you feel as though you are consistently being thrown towards one shoulder? Do you feel as though you are blocking the movement of the horse with one hip?

Saddlecloths and numnahs

The fit of anything under the saddle, such as protective pads or the saddlecloth, is also important for the comfort of the horse. Saddlecloths and pads that are shaped to accommodate the withers are less likely to cause pressure problems. If the saddlecloth moves when the horse is working, it may be that the cut of the cloth is unsuitable for the shape of the horse or that the saddle is not fitting correctly.

Shaped saddlecloths reduce the risk of pressure problems on the sensitive wither area

Rugs

Rugging issues often go hand-in-hand with concerns about being saddled and are generally linked to discomfort in the shoulders, withers and back. When a horse reacts to being rugged it is rarely simply a habit or the sign of a 'sour' horse; even horses that bite hard or kick out when rugged change dramatically when the source of the problem is addressed.

Even the best fitting rugs can cause problems for the horse when rolling or getting up. If possible, give your horse the opportunity to have some time either in the stable or in the field without the constraints of the rug. Rolling without a rug is extremely beneficial to the horse's back, skin and general wellbeing and helps him to release tension through his body after exercise or after a long period of standing in.

Even the best fitting rugs can restrict the horse when getting up from a roll

---

Rug wise

Check your rug fits by ensuring:

- there is plenty of room through the neck and shoulders to allow for movement.

- there is no pressure on the withers when the horse's head is down – the circumference of the base of the neck increases by several inches when a horse lowers his head.

- it does not pull back during the course of the day or night as this puts more pressure on the neck, withers and shoulders.

- it is long enough to sit comfortably over the hindquarters.

- it is deep enough to cover his body so that he is adequately protected from the cold and wet.

- the horse cannot catch a leg in it when getting up.

Feet

The hooves and feet can affect how the horse functions on a physical and mental level, and are influenced by diet, posture, training and management. The perfect foot, like the perfect horse, does not exist, but an awareness and understanding of your horse's feet will enable you to help him maintain mobility and increase his longevity.

The front feet provide stability and lateral balance during movement, with the hind feet providing centered balance. All feet provide drive. The front feet should be rounder than the hind feet since they perform a slightly different job. The hooves and teeth continue to grow after maturity. This means that they are in need of constant attention and it is a false economy to allow the feet to go untrimmed on a regular basis. Ideally the foot should receive professional attention every six weeks to minimize problems such as dropped heels and long toes. More frequent attention may be required if the horse is in need of significant re-balancing, such work must be done little by little and in conjunction with appropriate bodywork or other therapies to allow adjustments to the horse's posture to take place slowly and gradually.

As the foot is the basis for the whole skeletal structure of the horse, an imbalance in the hoof will affect how the energy created in the foot at the point of impact is transferred through the joints and soft tissue. Many problems such as sore shins, knees and hocks or tight shoulders, backs and hips can be traced to incorrect foot balance. Similarly tension through the back, shoulders and hindquarters as well as overall conformation of the limbs will affect the balance of the horse and the way his weight is distributed over the hooves. Simple observations can tell you whether the foot is balanced or not. The balanced foot should hit the ground reasonably level and the horse's weight should be distributed evenly through each hoof whether he is moving or standing still.

As with all aspects of equine management, foot

This shoe is crooked, the frog is uneven and the hoof wall is unlevel which will affect every joint

This foot is in better balance and the shoe is providing more even support

care does not take place in isolation. It is an extremely important part of the bigger picture, and it is as much the responsibility of the owner or trainer as it is the farrier to ensure that the horse's feet are the best that they can be. Since there is no such thing as the perfect foot, the aim should be to create as much balance as possible while taking into account the rest of the horse's posture and way he moves.

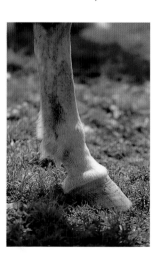

Long toes and under-run heels alter the balance and movement of the horse

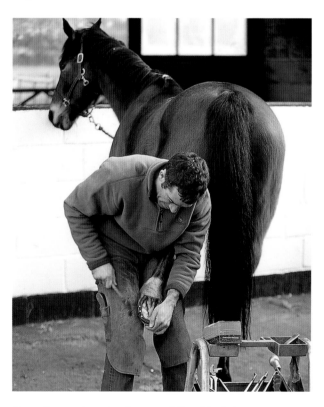

Correct foot care is not just the responsibility of the farrier

Teeth

Horses are under increasing pressure to perform bigger and better at a younger and younger age. Even horses destined for the pleasure market are often started at three years old. With adult teeth erupting from the ages of two through to five, this means that the horse is going through significant changes in the mouth at the exact time when he is being asked to accept a bit, move in balance and learn how to organize himself under saddle.

Retained caps and general dental changes can set up behavioural problems by causing discomfort, tension and imbalances through the still-growing body of the young equine. They can make it uncomfortable for youngsters to wear a headcollar or bridle. Comfort levels influence tolerance levels and many handling problems in horses of any age can be linked to problems within the oral cavity.

Dental issues that are overlooked as the horse matures can undermine his health by placing uneven stress on the ligaments and joints of the head, which will affect the rest of the body. In addition, common behavioural problems such as head-shaking, biting, rearing and napping can be linked to discomfort in the mouth.

The mouth is often a major factor in determining how the horse is able to perform. Tension patterns can be caused by and can contribute to dental problems. For example:

■ When a horse lowers his neck and head, the lower mandible (jaw bone) moves slightly forward. If the teeth have worn unevenly and have ramps or hooks on

The crooked jaw, puffy cheeks and lacklustre hair around this horse's face are signs of dental problems

This horse struggles on the right rein. The root of the problem was discovered in the mouth, which is totally out of balance

their surfaces, this movement will be restricted and he will not be able to work with a bit without opening his mouth.

■ Sharp edges or rims, missing or protuberant teeth and other dental imbalances may cause a horse to lean more on one rein than the other. This makes the weight distribution through the limbs uneven and incorrect muscle development will quickly follow. Gait irregularities will occur and the horse may be described as being bridle lame. Alternatively, he may work consistently behind the bit and may 'break' at the poll. Over-flexing decreases the flow of oxygen through the airways causing stress and fatigue.

■ Long or sharp canine teeth and wolf teeth can interfere with the bit action and damage the tongue. They may cause sudden and extreme pain giving rise to volatile, explosive behaviour. They can be responsible for a horse's reluctance to move forward freely from the leg and cause bridling and bitting issues.

It is important to recognize that the oral balance of a horse's mouth can be affected through poor rider posture, poor saddle and bit fit, certain feeding regimes and incorrect training techniques. Regular dental check-ups are vital for the overall health of the horse.

The bony lump on the bottom jaw (present on both sides) is due to deciduous teeth that did not shed correctly. Not surprisingly, this pony is impossible to catch and is now in rescue where he will receive appropriate help

Regular dental check-ups are vital for the horse's wellbeing

Rider and handler posture

Rider posture influences and is influenced by the balance of the horse, saddle fit, dental wear, muscle development and physical performance. To ensure that the rider has the best chance of achieving some degree of symmetry there needs to be as much potential for balance as possible. A crooked rider will create a crooked horse and vice versa.

Slouching or hollowing the back, dropping one hip, raising or fixing a hand, tightening or raising a shoulder, tilting the pelvis forward or back and consistently looking down are just some of the postural habits that occur in riders. All of these traits affect the horse and encourage uneven muscle development. Similarly, if the horse is uneven, the rider will compensate for the horse and so the cycle continues.

Dropping the hip will encourage uneven rein contact and restrict movement through the hindquarter

Of course, eyes from the ground are invaluable but even without the help of another person you can bring about improvements to your posture by making small adjustments to where your feet are placed on the stirrup bars, the position of your pelvis, by padding up a saddle on an unevenly muscled horse, or by improving your balance through working on the ground with your horse.

Riding with the base of the toes on the stirrup bar causes tension through the rider and the horse

Riding with the ball of the foot on the stirrup prevents the rider from bracing through the hips and allows the horse's back to lengthen and lift

Hollowing the back...

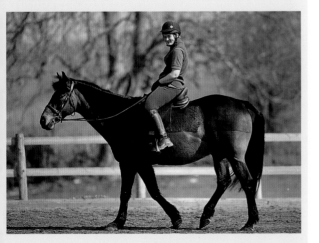

...or slouching pushes the horse onto the forehand and restricts movement through his back

A person who is out of balance when leading a horse will inadvertently encourage the horse to walk on the forehand, brace in the neck and/or lean slightly towards the handler thus developing habits that are harder to alter once the horse is under saddle. Simple exercises for horse and rider can help improve the balance of both, and by being aware of your own postural habits and making steps to change them, you can begin to make a dramatic difference to the way the horse moves.

If his handler is out of balance, a horse will compensate and uneven muscle development and movement will quickly develop

Assess your horse

There are three main ways to start the assessment process: look, listen and feel. If you are not accustomed to studying horses in this way, start with some simple points such as head carriage and the way your horse holds his tail. Don't be disheartened if things don't jump out at you straight away. Like all aspects of horse care, assessment requires practice and some people are naturally more adept at using their eyes than others. Make notes on a daily or weekly basis, be open-minded and above all stay positive. Far from looking at him critically, the aim is to get to know and understand your horse on a whole new level. By becoming aware of his usual habits you will know when they have changed.

Look – postural observations

Try to get into the habit of spending time simply observing your horse. Keep your eyes soft by using your peripheral vision rather than simply staring. Watch the horse for a moment and then blink or look away. This often enables you to see more. Although you may notice a lot at first, keep checking in with the horse to ensure that this is a true pattern and not just the way he is moving or standing at that particular moment.

Watch how he moves around his stable, and his general posture when at rest. When loose in the field, look for free easy movement in a good rhythm and balance with an equal length and height of stride in both hind and forelimbs. Look at the muscle development through his face, neck, chest, back and hindquarters. Is it equal on both sides, or are some parts more developed on one side?

Watch how he stands. Is he square or does he stand in an uneven frame with one foreleg or one hind leg forward

This mare is bracing through the base of the neck and shoulders, even when moving in the field

This horse is also tight through the shoulders and back – the lack of top line in front of the wither indicates that he habitually moves in a high-headed posture

or behind? Does he always rest the same hind leg? Does he stand with his forelimbs wide apart and his hind limbs together or vice versa?

Front view

Look at your horse head-on while he is standing. Look at his muzzle. Are his nostrils level or does one appear to be higher than the other? Is his jaw straight or does he hold his lower jaw out to one side? Does he tilt his nose more to the left or right or is his head straight? Are his ears the same height when in the same position?

Uneven ears are linked to tension through the jaw and poll

(Above) Otto is base wide in front and base narrow behind, which is linked to tension through the lumbar area and hindquarter

Look at his forequarters. Does his neck bulge more on one side than the other? Is one shoulder flatter or more developed than the other? Does he stand with one foreleg out to the side or does he stand with his weight more on one leg than the other? Are his front limbs straight?

(Right) Note how the horse stands. Persistent resting of the same hindleg relates to how this horse disconnects through the back and hindquarters and is linked to the diagonal shoulder in some cases

(Right) This mare has uneven nostrils and carries her muzzle slightly to the left

Note the uneven nostrils and muzzle, protruding cheekbones and unlevel ears

(Below) Fleur has twisted front limbs and habitually stands with her left fore out to the side. Not surprisingly she finds it hard to bring her front legs forward for the farrier

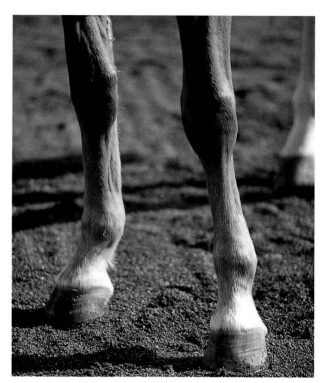

This mare is weighting her right fore more than the left

Does he turn his toes out or is he pigeon-toed? Is his weight evenly distributed through the middle of the front limb or does he bear the weight on the inside or outside of the limb? To check if the weight is even, stand in front of your horse and draw an imaginary line from the point of the shoulder down the front limb. The line should pass down the centre of the forearm, straight through the knee, down the cannon bone and cut the hoof in half. If the limb is not straight or if the hoof is unlevel, the imaginary line will not bisect the limb and hoof, meaning that the horse bears more weight on one side of the foot than the other. Draw another imaginary line across the front of the hoof from one point of the coronary band to the other – the line should be parallel to the ground indicating that the coronary band is even on both sides. If one side of the coronary band is significantly higher or lower, the foot is uneven.

Look at the front hooves. Are they even and a pair, or is one hoof more upright? Do the hooves flare at any point? Look at the rings on the hooves. Check whether they are evenly formed and run parallel around the hoof or drop or rise at a steeper angle nearer the heel.

Pick up each foot and check whether the hoof wall is even all the way round or whether it rises or drops on the inside or outside off the foot. Look at the bars. Are they

This horse has twisted front limbs

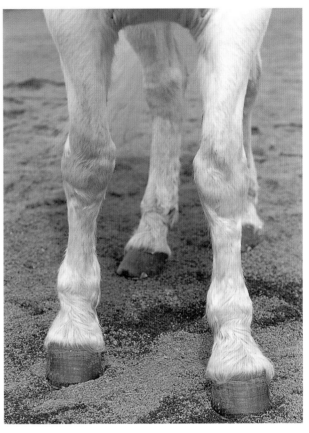

This horse is unlevel with her weight distributed unevenly through the front limbs. She is carrying more weight on her right forelimb – if a plumb line was taken from the point of the shoulder, it would fall more to the inside of the limb

straight or bent? Are they weak or over-developed? Check that the frog is symmetrical. An uneven or misshapen frog can be indicative of an uneven foot.

Look at the hind hooves in the same way.

These hooves have not received appropriate care and are flared, putting uneven strain on the pasterns, which has a knock-on effect through the rest of the body

Check the balance of the foot and the shape of the frog

Wellington – Part One

Wellington, a TBX, was born in 1990 and originally trained for dressage. Purchased at 14 years old as a cheap project horse by his current owner, Wellington came with the reputation of being a kicker and a biter and not for the faint-hearted. For instance, he could only be tacked up and groomed in cross ties. The vendor had wisely turned down offers from two novice horse owners as there were so many things that Wellington could not tolerate. In some situations, he would be dangerous.

Wellington arrived at Tilley Farm in July 2004. His reputation had not been exaggerated. He was aggressive around food, couldn't stand still, couldn't halt in hand or under saddle, couldn't walk in a straight line, bit, kicked out, squealed, and struck. He was territorial and could not be skipped out or approached when he was still in his stable. When eating Wellington would snatch a mouthful of food, then stop and drool. He was extremely odour-sensitive and any supplements in his feed were viewed with suspicion.

Wellington was so incorrectly muscled that he found it impossible to lower his head

His posture was so uneven that every part of his body was out of balance. His neck was crooked and his hooves were totally unbalanced. He carried his weight on his left fore and habitually held his neck high with his head tilted. His belly was carried significantly out to the right, while the sacroiliac joint was visible and unlevel. There was significant loss of articulation through the right hock. His eye was almond-shaped and sour-looking and he could not tolerate any contact on the upper part of the neck. Tight necks can cause major problems if the horse needs to be injected and Wellington absolutely exploded screaming, striking and trying to double-barrel our vet when he had to be sedated for a thorough dental check. Fortunately, everyone was prepared and we had the added benefit of having the best and the fastest vet in the West although it has to be said I have never seen a person go quite that colour before!

Under saddle Wellington could only work with a high head carriage and would fling his neck higher when asked for any transition. He would swish his tail and cow kick against the rider's leg and lateral movement was non-existent. Wellington was so incorrectly muscled that it was hardly surprising that he was one unhappy horse. In spite of this, bizarrely, he did seem to enjoy his work, and so the long road back to recovery began. (Concluded on p.102.)

Side view

Look at both sides of the horse, keeping a mental picture of one side when you move to the other. Does he tend to stand with his head up or down? Does his mane change directions or does it lie easily to one side? Does his back drop or is it level and well covered? Can you see the spinous processes of the backbone? Is he level, croup high or built 'up hill'? Are his hindquarters rounded or does he have bony projections such as a jumper's bump? Is the muscling even on both sides? Is there muscle wastage, excessive or incorrect muscle development? Does the ribcage and back fill slightly as he breathes in or is the movement restricted to the abdomen?

Bailey lacks muscle over his top line, and his withers and croup are prominent

Fish broke his pelvis when he was young; the bony lump just above his tail (inset, left) is evidence of this damage

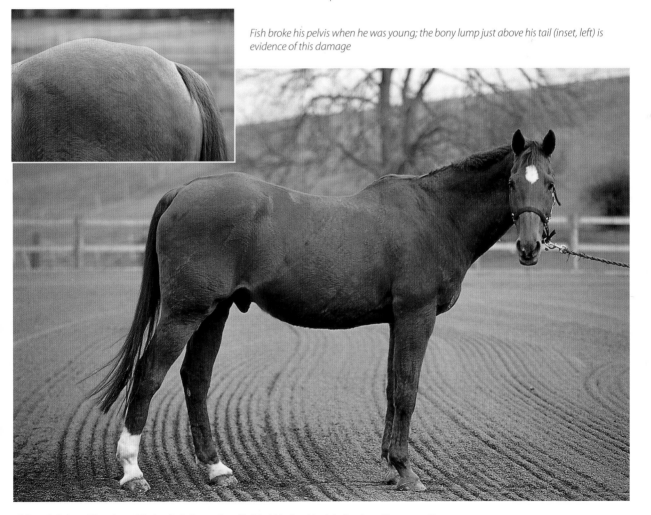

Although Fish is old and part TB, the dip in front of and behind his shoulder is indicative of long-standing incorrect posture rather than age or breed type

Assess your horse

Does he stand evenly with a leg at each corner or does he stand with his front limbs or hind limbs underneath him or strung out? Note whether the heel is at the same angle to the toes or whether it is under run or more upright. Check to see whether the slope of the pastern is similar to that of the hoof.

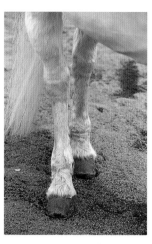

These hooves are out of balance – there is a marked difference between the angle of the pastern and the slope of the hoof wall. This is putting strain on the pasterns and fetlocks

Horses that stand with the hindquarters twisted and the hind limbs at an angle are often tight or lack awareness through the loins

(Above) Bertie has a clamped tail, which is linked to over-development of muscle through the shoulder. He also habitually stands with his right hind forward and his right fore back

(Below) This mare is over-developed through the forequarters and is strung out behind, consistent with a horse that has worked habitually on the forehand and struggles with engagement

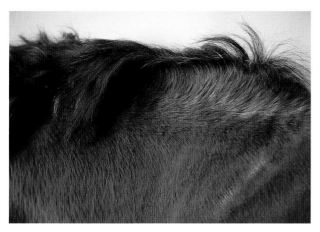

The mane changes direction where there is a swirl or where tension is present; at the wither it will generally fall to the lower shoulder

Note the slight mane change in front of the wither, which corresponds to the over-developed muscle in front of the shoulder. This mare is already starting to build more top line but her shoulders are still more developed than her hindquarters

Otto – Part One

Otto is a warmblood and was born in 1991. Sired by Jolie Coeur, Otto was bought by me as a weanling but sadly fell as a youngster and damaged a hip joint. He had three months box rest and was treated by my vet and chartered

physiotherapist. From then on it seemed we were taking two steps forward and one back all the time. He had times when he was well and times when I wondered whether we were doing the right thing in keeping him going. With such an injury it was important that he was worked consistently to keep up muscle tone around the vulnerable hip area but finding the right combination of groundwork and ridden work was challenging. The damage was permanent. It affected his entire body; tension through the neck, left shoulder, midback and lumbar area were inevitable as a knock-on effect from the pelvic damage.

There is always a reason for unwanted behaviour and Otto was a perfect illustration of this fact. When sore, he would nip, fidget and barge, and at nearly 17hh he could become quite difficult to handle at times. He would also be understandably inconsistent under saddle and would either work like a dream or spook, drop a shoulder and spin, dumping new riders to the ground. (Concluded on p.83.)

Rear view

Standing behind your horse, look at the tail. Is it low set or high set? Is it straight or does it kink to one side, either from the top of the dock or further down the tailbone? Is it clamped in the tail groove or is it relaxed? Can the horse stand straight or does he hold his neck persistently to one side? Is he base narrow (stands with his feet close together) or base wide (stands with his feet wide apart)? Is his pelvis level or is it higher on one side? Are the hind limbs straight or is he cow-hocked? If your horse is quiet and non-reactive to movement behind him, you can look down on him by standing on a box. You can then make further observations on how he is muscled through the neck, back and hindquarters.

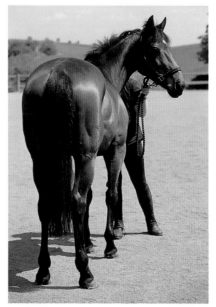

If a horse appears to be cow-hocked or twists through the hind limbs it may be due to tension through the loins and pelvis and is not necessary simply a conformation fault

Note the level of the hindquarters and the angle of the hind limbs – here the left hip is significantly higher than the right hip

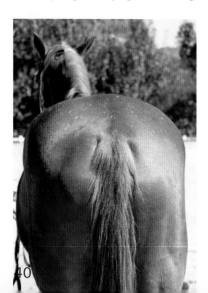

This mare is higher on the left side of her pelvis and her hindquarters have developed unevenly. Note how the tail follows the same pattern – the top of the tail appears higher on the left

If safe to do so, stand on a box and look along the horse's back. You will be able to make more observations and will be able to see how the shoulders differ. Nokia's right shoulder is lower and flatter than the left shoulder

On the move

Ask a friend to lead the horse away from you and towards you. Then ask them to lead him past you on both sides.

Watch how he tracks up. When heading straight towards you, does his head tilt to one side? Can you see more of his barrel on one side or is it even? In some horses an uneven barrel is obvious, even when stationary as the belly sticks out more to one side than the other. When heading away from you, are his hindquarters level or does he drop one hip lower than the other?

Ask someone to walk your horse away from you...

...and towards you

Watch the limbs for even movement. Do the fetlocks flex evenly or does one fetlock sink more or less than the others? Do both hocks articulate evenly or does one hind leg look stiffer and straighter than the other? When the feet hit the ground, do they land squarely or does one side land first? Do any of the limbs twist? Does the horse move effortlessly through the shoulder or does he lead with the knee? Is the stride even with both fore limbs or hind limbs covering the same amount of ground? Does the horse lift each hoof off the ground at an equal height?

Does he always lead with the same leg when moving off from a halt? Does he appear to be 'holding' or bracing in his poll, neck, back or hindquarters? Does he take a hind limb towards the midline?

PRACTISE HORSE WATCHING

There are endless observations to be made when watching your horse, and detecting the smaller more subtle patterns of tension takes experience. You can increase your awareness by practising with a horse that you don't know as well as you may know your own horse. It can be hard to start looking at your horse in an objective way and can be easier to note postural traits when you are less biased about what you might see. The more you watch, the more you will learn and the easier it will be to spot any peculiarities such as a tendency to roll or lie on one side in the field or stable or being concerned when approached in certain directions by other horses or humans.

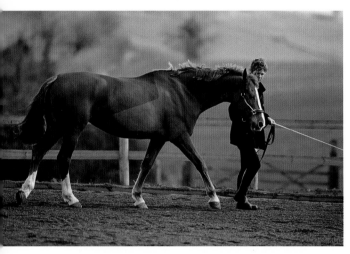

Watch the quality of movement. Easta is a little tight through the shoulders, which will reduce her ability to engage

(Below) Baron is blocked through the body and lacks impulsion. Even walking looks like an effort

Handling and day-to-day care

When handling your horse, note how he reacts to being caught, turned out, tied up, led, asked to stand, saddled, bridled, rugged up, groomed, washed off, having his feet picked up and being shod. Note how he eats. Is he grumpy and defensive around food? Does he chew on one side, drop feed or take a few mouthfuls and then drool? Does he eat calmly, hesitantly or bolt his food?

More information can be gleaned by looking for other indicators of uneven tension such as excessively or unevenly worn shoes or hooves, rugs that always slip to the same side or rub marks from the bridle (including the reins), saddle or rug. When untacking or changing rugs, look for any hair on the inside of the rug or under the saddle pad. More hair will collect where there is more pressure from the material. Ill-fitting rugs and tack can be a big contributor to physical problems (see pp.20–26). If the middle of the saddle pad is significantly cleaner than its front and back, this may indicate a bridging saddle. More dirt or hair on one side of the saddle pad may also be indicative of a crooked horse, saddle and/or rider.

Check saddle cloths, saddle panels and rugs for grease and hair to see where there is greater pressure. This pattern of dirt and hair shows that the rider is sitting on the back of the saddle and that the saddle is bridging. This can cause issues with saddling, loss of muscle, lack of engagement, and in some cases bucking and bolting

(Above) Harley was concerned about having his feet washed. He was also worried about contact on the lower leg and extremely agitated when being shod. By doing TTouches on his legs (see p.79) we were able to help him overcome all of his concerns and within a week we could handle his legs with ease

Rugs will generally slip to the lower side of the horse

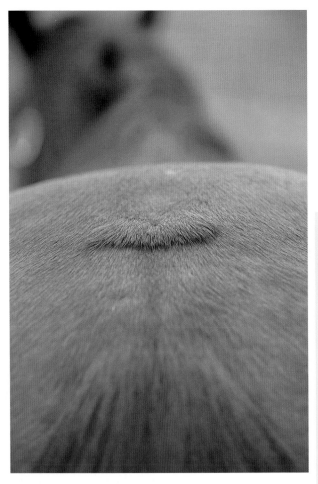

Raised hair is a sign that something is rubbing

Check the rug or coat for stable stains and mud. If only ever present on one side it may mean that your horse favours rolling or lying on one side. Check the bedding and stable walls as well to learn more about your horse. Dirt and grease on the stable walls can mean that the horse is sitting on the walls to relieve tension through the lumbar area and if the beautiful deep, high banked bed that you laboured over for hours is reduced to a scene reminiscent of trench warfare overnight it may mean that your horse finds it hard to settle and relax in his stable.

If your horse favours rolling on one side...

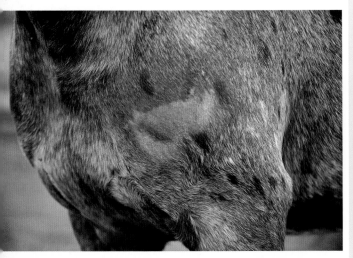

A rug that slips backwards will rub the shoulders and cause tension through the chest, shoulders and withers

...it may mean that he is unable to roll right over, indicating tension through the back or that he is significantly stiffer on one side

Condition

The skin and coat say a lot about the health of a horse. A happy horse in good condition and with plenty of vitality should have a smooth, glossy coat with a natural shine. A dry, staring coat generally indicates that the horse is in some degree of pain, is deficient in vital nutrients or is unwell and should be seen by a vet. Smaller changes in the coat provide more information. Dandruff, scurf, raised hair, coarse patches, and certain skin conditions can be linked to areas of tension or blocked awareness in his body. Temperature changes may also be evident: hot patches generally indicate an acute problem and cold patches a chronic problem. Changes in the direction of the lay of the hair can be indicative of tight skin and muscles.

Note where the horse sweats and how his coat dries when wet. Old injuries to the neck and withers in particular can lead to patches of sweat in specific areas on the side of the neck or on a shoulder and, of course, white marks on the coat or mane generally indicate old damage from rugs, hoods or saddles. The coat will dry more quickly where there is more heat and stay wetter where there is less circulation although normal sweat patterns must, of course, be taken into consideration. When his coat is changing in spring and autumn, note any areas that take longer to change. The winter coat may hang on in areas where circulation to the skin is impaired. In some cases, the horse may never shed completely in specific areas. Persistent itching in the same area can be another sign of blocked awareness.

It is also worth noting where flies gather on the horse. While they obviously tend to gather around the eye to obtain water, other very specific areas where flies congregate, such as on the midline or over the kidneys or even on a limb, can indicate congestion.

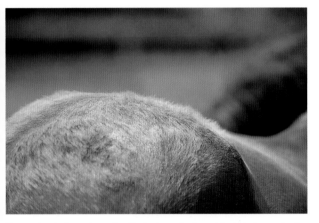

Dry staring hair can be a sign that a horse lacks nutrients but can also be attributed to areas where the skin is tight

Persistent scratching can be a sign of blocked awareness or tension

Otto is always tighter through the right lumbar area due to an accident as a youngster and his winter coat is coarser here than anywhere else on his body

White patches on the mane and/or coat can be indicative of damage from ill fitting equipment

Listen

Listening to your horse can make you more aware of how he is feeling, particularly if something suddenly changes. Problems with wind, such as roaring, are obvious and should be discussed with your vet but some horses that are tight through the throat latch area and work consistently behind the vertical also make a noise that could indicate they are struggling, particularly if it only happens at certain times under saddle. Grunting when passing droppings or getting up, frequent shallow sighing and grinding or scraping teeth may also indicate that the horse is uncomfortable or concerned. Listen for the footfall of the horse when walking him in hand or riding. Is it even or does one hoof land more heavily than the others? Does he drag his hind feet on the surface or scuff the ground with his front feet? Does he forge?

Dragging a toe or scuffing the ground is a sign that the horse lacks impulsion through that limb

Feel

In addition to using your powers of observation use a flat hand exploration to confirm your thoughts or to give you a more specific idea about where the areas of tension lie. Start at the poll and run the palm of your hand smoothly down the neck and shoulder. Run your hand under the neck, down the shoulder, along the barrel, flank, stomach, over the back and hindquarters and down all four limbs ensuring that you check every part of your horse on both sides of his body. Check for ticklish areas, hot or cold patches, muscle spasm, coarse hair, over- or under-developed muscles, or a feeling of tightness in the skin. If you are unable to gauge any changes, try doing the exploration with the back of your hand.

Harley – Part One

Harley is a five-year-old Appaloosa gelding purchased from a local horse fair. Bought to sell on, Harley was proving rather difficult to handle in certain situations and was being seen by one of our practitioners-in-training, Cat Wilton, as a case study.

Harley was very headshy and was therefore difficult to bridle. He was tense through almost every part of his body and had hot patches over the poll and cooler areas over the loins, hindquarters and lower legs. He was jumpy, disliked being touched and could not tolerate any contact on his legs. This understandably made him hard to shoe, as he would strike out with his front legs. When lunged by his owner, his hind limbs would slip outwards. He could only be mounted by being put into a corner to inhibit his ability to move away and he would turn his quarters when anyone entered his stable. When his owner injured her back, Harley came to Tilley Farm for two weeks. (Concluded on p.124.)

(Above) Run the flat of your hand over your horse's body, feeling for changes in temperature, coat texture and muscle quality

(Right) Check for 'ticklish' spots and areas that cause concern for the horse – stay relaxed and refrain from punishing the horse if he appears defensive or worried

Run your hand lightly over your horse's face, jowls and ears. It is preferable to use the back of your hand as this is less invasive. If your horse is unsure about having his head handled, stand to one side, otherwise do this checking from in front. Support the noseband of the headcollar lightly with one hand and run the other hand up over the forehead and then down the nasal bone. Are the muscles

It is more likely that he has always been uncomfortable about contact in that part of his body. Pain, fear and fear of pain will usually trigger the same response.

If your horse is happy to be handled around the hindquarters and tail, check the tail for tension. Can you lift it from the tail grove? Is he defensive about having his tail touched? Does the tail quiver when you lift it from the

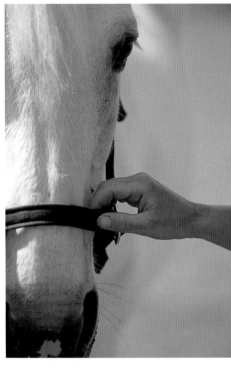

Support the headcollar lightly by resting your fingers on the noseband...

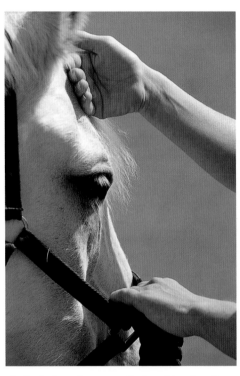

...and run the back of your fingers over the horse's head and face

on the forehead even, bulging or is one side more developed than the other? Run your fingertips gently down either side of the jaw checking for any reaction that may indicate dental problems.

Be completely honest about how your horse reacts to contact. Note whether he pulls faces when you touch a certain area, pins his ears, hardens his eyes or holds his breath (see pp.16–19). He may move away, lift a leg, fidget, headshake or nip to express his concern. Even if he has always reacted to being touched around the girth area, for example, this does not mean that is 'just the way he is'.

tail groove? Is it stiff all the way down? Is it floppy? Does it kink at any point? Does the end of the tail bone curl up or twist to one side?

With your hand on the withers, gently rock the horse away from you and then guide him gently back to you. Is the movement easy or does he struggle to transfer his weight when being asked to move to the left or right?

One final check is to lift each leg in turn. Run your hand down the back of the leg you want to pick up and ask the horse to pick up his leg by giving a little squeeze and release on the tendon. Note whether your horse snatches the leg up or whether he lifts it readily. Does he lean on you once you are supporting the limb? Is one limb heavier than the other? If you can, also note how long it takes the horse to organize his body in such a way that he can lift

Lift the tail from the tail groove. Harley is tight through the tail and the first two thirds of his tail are rigid, linking to tension in his shoulders and back

Rock the withers to see how easy it is (or isn't) for the horse to transfer his weight effortlessly through the shoulders and front limbs

If the horse is tight through the pelvis, he may shake a hind limb and lift the leg higher than normal. Go with the movement and then slowly lower the leg

This horse's tail is also stiff but this time it is carried away from the body like a rod

the leg. Some horses will need to place the diagonal hind toe on the ground before a forelimb is lifted. Others may need to straddle the other limbs first. Can the horse stand easily on three legs or does he hop about or try to snatch the leg back out of your hand? Does the hind limb shake when you hold it? Does he slam the leg back down or can he lower it slowly and evenly until the foot is back on the ground?

Under saddle

Generally a horse will behave the same way under saddle as he does in hand. A high-headed horse that spins wildly around the handler when being led is likely to be a rather lively if not alarming ride. A horse that dislikes being lead or approached from the offside may find it hard to work on the right rein.

As you walk, feel for freedom of movement in both you and your horse. Asking someone to lead your horse for you, while you close your eyes may help you to become more aware of his pattern of movement. Does he throw you forward and to one side or is the movement even? Even though your stirrup leathers are the same length, does one feel longer than the other? Do you feel straight or do you feel as though you are dropping to one side or twisting in the saddle? Do you feel behind or ahead of the movement? Are your legs in the same position or does one feel as if it is sliding forward or back?

When hacking or schooling, be aware of points such as over-sensitivity or resistance to leg aids, difficulty in striking off on a particular lead, hollowing, rushing, planting, napping or stiffness on a particular rein. Does he lean on the bit or throw his head in the air? Does he buck when asked to canter or after a jump? Does he tighten his back and swish his tail when asked for an upward transition? When walking in a straight line look down at his shoulders and note whether they both move forward and back to the same degree or whether one is more restricted in its range of movement. Jigging, rearing, rushing fences, stumbling, spooking, bucking, hollowing the back, swinging away as you mount, or sluggish movement can all indicate uneven tension.

The posture of the horse in hand will be the same under saddle and...

...high-headed horses are more likely to be spooky and flight-oriented

Under saddle be aware of how the horse moves. Hollowing, rushing...

...and leaning are signs of tension through the neck and back

After you dismount check whether you have any aches or pain. If, for example, you have discomfort in your lower back during or after riding it is likely that your horse is carrying tension through the lumbar region as well. If you ride several horses you may be aware of a different pattern of holding for each horse.

Even if you are simply hacking be aware of how you feel through the body and try to match any areas of tension in your body to how the horse is moving beneath you

Fish – Part One

Born in March 1982, Fish is a chestnut Anglo Arab who was bought by his current owner, Mags Denness, when he was six months old. He was sent away to be started as a three-year-old but went up and over backwards with the trainer, causing permanent damage to his sacrum and tail base. He did, however, go on to compete successfully in Riding Club activities and BHS eventing and completed one intermediate event before Mags went to university. Fish was then hacked and hunted. At the age of 15 he was moved to the West Country.

Fish had always been high-headed, spooky, tight in the neck, reactive and overly sensitive to changes in his routine. He had a tendency to form very strong attachments to other horses and would be visibly depressed when Mags was away. His behaviour would escalate if he was upset. He would become highly agitated, go off his feed and had no ability to self-calm.

Fish arrived at Tilley Farm in 2002 aged 19. He had muscle wastage and a non-existent top line primarily from poor saddle fit. Old injuries and age were not on his side but there was room for improvement to guarantee some quality of life for this intelligent, willing and very sweet-natured horse. (Concluded on p.120.)

Interpreting what you find

Horses that are highly defensive about being handled or protective about their stable and/or paddock are often tight through their whole body. Others may have more specific areas of tension. Once you have made your general observations, study the various parts of the horse's anatomy in greater detail to check more thoroughly for areas of tension or weakness.

in the mouth is reduced. Working around the mouth, both inside and out stimulates the salivary glands and also triggers the relaxation-promoting parasympathetic nervous system (see p.13). This quietens the sympathetic nervous system, responsible for the 'fight, flight or freeze' responses (pp.18–19).

Tension around the mouth generally signifies an overly emotional and sensitive horse. It inhibits breathing,

Horses that are sensitive or defensive about being handled are often tight through the whole body

Mouth work helps to improve focus and behaviour

Mouth, muzzle and chin

The mouth is linked to learning. When humans concentrate, they may chew pens or fingertips or lick or bite their lips. Babies of any mammal species often place items in their mouths and a recent study on the learning process in children in Manchester, UK, has concluded that children retain more information when they are chewing gum as they learn.

The mouth is also linked to the limbic system, the area of the brain considered to be the control centre for the emotions and the gateway to learning (this is described in detail by Daniel Goleman in his book *Emotional Intelligence*). This emotional connection is consistent with observations made by Linda Tellington Jones (see p.5) that many horses improve in their behaviour and their ability to operate in a calm and focused way once tension

Tension around the mouth can be a sign of a sensitive horse

which may be light and shallow, and is linked to a state of tension existing throughout the entire body. If the mouth feels really tight the horse may be inclined to reject tidbits.

Horses with a **very short mouth** can be slow to mature both mentally and emotionally. They may also have a very short concentration span and will need time to process information. Lessons, whether in hand or under saddle, may need to be repeated over and over again – owners or trainers of small-mouthed horses can become extremely frustrated as they may feel they are forever taking two steps forward and one back. However, training can be tailored to keep such horses stimulated, interested and thinking, without overloading them mentally and emotionally. In this case, several short training sessions throughout the day are more beneficial to both horse and owner/carer than one long one. Working around and inside the mouth can help change the pattern of holding in this area enabling the horse to increase his concentration span and retain more information.

Billy has a short mouth and a short concentration span to match. His mouth movements are hurried...

...and he carries tension through the chin and muzzle

Jack – Part One

Jack lives at the Episkopi Saddle Club in Cyprus. The club is based in an area known as Happy Valley, and for the way the horses are cared for here, never mind any of its other attributes, the place deserves its name. Jack is a little bay ex-racehorse and, like so many horses in Cyprus, bears the scars of some pretty rough handling. He attended my first TTEAM workshop on the island with his carer Michelle.

One of the most obvious things about Jack was his tongue, which lolled pretty consistently out to the side. His eyes were rather dull, and he also had white marks across the top of his poll and more on the underside of his neck by the throat latch area. Apparently, Jack had sustained these injuries while being loaded into a trailer before being taken in by the Saddle Club. A chain had been placed around the top of his neck and he had been literally dragged into the trailer by a tractor. It is possible that this had damaged the hyoid bone, which would have explained the lolling tongue, and was probably linked to the bizarre behaviour Jack displayed when standing in his corral. He had developed a habit of throwing his head over the fence, pressing down the upper part of his throat and curling his neck over the rail at the throat latch while wind sucking. He would do this over and over in a mindless way unless he was occupied with eating, after which he would resume the activity. He was also incredibly insecure and would become stressed if no other horses were around. He couldn't be taken into the yard to be saddled and couldn't be left tied up on his own.

In spite of it all Jack was a sweet horse and I abhor such unnecessary and inappropriate handling. However, you can't always know when or why something changed for a horse. Pity can limit your potential to see a positive outcome, so it is best not to dwell on a horse's previous experiences. You have to meet the horse where he is at the current time, work accordingly and do what you can. Michelle primarily wanted Jack to be as comfortable and relaxed as possible and to enjoy the bodywork. Anything else that followed as a result of the session would be a bonus. (Concluded on p.140.)

If the **bottom lip is permanently floppy**, it does not mean that the horse is relaxed. It can be an indication of discomfort and tension in the poll area and may be indicative of long standing dental problems. Horses with this type of lower lip can be prone to sudden explosive behaviour. They can suddenly bolt or over-react and then come back down to earth as though nothing had happened. By freeing up the tension in the poll and bringing awareness to the lower lip, the volatile outbursts can be reduced and in some cases disappear altogether.

A tight muzzle is often accompanied by **tight or pinched nostrils and hard eyes**. Tight nostrils can be linked to a lack of tolerance and aloof and disinterested behaviour. Contributory factors such as dental problems should be addressed.

The **tongue and saliva** can also be an indicator of stress. Thick, sticky, white saliva can be linked to poor gut function and may be caused by carbohydrate overload while a dry mouth may be an indicator of a nervous horse. Tongue chewing, lolling or sucking can be a sign of discomfort. If your horse constantly sucks or pokes his tongue, or constantly chews on things even when at rest it is worth conducting a thorough physical examination. Hormonal imbalances can also give rise to mouth issues.

A soft bottom lip can be a sign that the horse is relaxed...

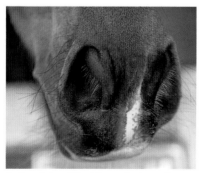

...but a permanently floppy lip is a sign of often significant tension through the poll

(Left and above) Nostrils vary in size and shape and can give you information about the horse's levels of tolerance

INDICATORS OF TENSION IN THE MOUTH

Horses that hold tension through the mouth and muzzle area can also be:

- Difficult to paste worm
- Reluctant to tolerate dental work
- Difficult to catch and/or bridle
- Inclined to hold onto the bit when ridden or set their jaw against rein contact
- Easily distracted
- Headshy
- Likely to bite, nip or mouth
- Constantly worried
- Sharp to handle and ride
- Fussy eaters
- Aggressive around food
- Above or behind the vertical under saddle
- Clingy to other horses

Face, forehead and TMJ (temporomandibular joint)

The face, head and muzzle are among the most neglected parts of the horse yet so much information about the animal's wellbeing and character can be gleaned by studying them. The head and TMJ influence and are influenced by the tongue, poll, neck, shoulders, chest, back and hindquarters.

Horses that lack trust are generally **wary of contact around the head and face** and may be reactive to things moving towards them. They may have cold patches over the nasal bone and their breath may feel cold on your hand. This is sometimes evident in horses that regularly spook although it can also be found occasionally in more laidback horses. It is often accompanied by tension or hollowing in the wither area.

Bumps or ridges along the bottom of the jaw or down the face can be indicative of dental problems such as retained deciduous teeth. In young racehorses the appearance of bumps or sensitivity to the noseband on the bridle and headcollar can be linked to sudden tiring while galloping. Airflow through the nostrils may be reduced by as much as 60 per cent by the upper teeth not erupting properly due to unshed caps. Oral discomfort can also be linked to poor or uneven muscle development around the muzzle, jowl, face and forehead.

Some **facial conformation** is linked to certain characteristics. For example, dish-faced horses are often more sensitive and emotional than those with broader, flatter faces. The presence of a bony ridge between or just below the eyes can indicate that the horse may be slow to learn, resistant to pressure or quirky in his behaviour. While such horses can make great competition horses in the right hands, they may be unsuitable for a nervous handler as they often respond better to quiet consistent training. (For more details read *Getting in TTouch* by Linda Tellington Jones.)

Dished-faced horses are often more sensitive than horses with a straighter face – the greater the dish, the greater the sensitivity

Bumps on the bottom jaw or down the face can be linked to dental problems

A bony ridge between or just below the eye can indicate the horse may be slow to learn or resistant to pressure

Uneven protruding cheekbones can be due to an accident or congenital problem

Tension around the head can be present in horses that are anxious and worry over even small changes to routine or those that are in a constant state of alert. In horses that have suffered stress, the **area above each eye will be more indented.** Referred to as stress dips, such indents have little or nothing to do with age and can be apparent in very young horses. Uneven development of the temporal muscles or trauma to the head, jaw and face can cause issues with bridling and generally make a horse resistant on one rein. Evidence of an accident may be seen in significant changes to the TMJ, uneven protruding cheekbones, a thickened jowl, missing teeth or a fractured jaw or skull.

Tension in the TMJ can be linked to dental problems. If the horse has worked in a high-headed posture for some time, he may also be uncomfortable in this joint as this posture inhibits movement of the lower mandible. Checking the joint on both sides by feeling the area with your fingers can provide vital information about how a horse performs under saddle. In horses with an inability to work on a particular rein, a change can often be felt in the space or bone development on one side of the TMJ, which will often also result in problems with the opposite hip. Alternatively, damage to the hip and pelvis can result in an ongoing problem with the jaw, making regular dental checks vital as the teeth are more likely to wear unevenly.

Tension around the TMJ and poll can also prevent the horse moving forward freely from the leg, and working in a soft, rounded outline. It inhibits the horse's ability to arch his neck, affects balance and proprioception and will have a knock-on effect through the entire body.

Over-developed temporal muscles can indicate anxiety

Tension around the TMJ and poll can prevent the horse moving freely forward in the correct outline

Eyes

Along with his other senses, the horse uses sight to glean information about his surroundings. As humans tend to be less visually aware than animals, we can sometimes perceive horses as stupid or stubborn if they go into freeze, spook or rush when something in their environment has changed or is unfamiliar.

The conformation and placement of the eyes can determine how easily the horse is able to process visual information. Some horses, for example, have **eyes that are hooded** and there may be a bony bump on the face between them. Visual balance is impaired in horses with **eyes set to the side with large hooded lids** and they may find it hard to move forward in a consistent frame. When looking head-on at a horse with this type of conformation, you may not be able to see much of the eye. To be able to see in front of him, the horse may have to tighten the muscles across his forehead and upper lid, as well as raising his head, causing tension through the upper part of his neck. This type of eye can be the cause of erratic, spooky behaviour in some horses. They may happily pass an object three times but panic the fourth time.

Small eyes can be indicative of a horse that is more likely to be concerned about movement behind or around him. The eye may appear hard and the horse may seem permanently on the defensive. As with the horse with the hooded eye, the small-eyed horse may have a limited ability to process visual information due to the placement of the eye and the conformation of the head. He may find it hard to move forward, either in hand or under saddle, and may plant or move backwards when concerned.

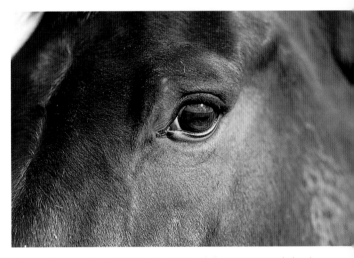

Horses with a small eye can be more concerned about movement behind or around them...

The eye's conformation and placement influences behaviour. Little of this horse's eye can be seen from in front...

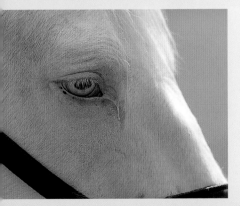

...in order to look ahead, he has to tighten the muscles around the eyelid

...and may be spooky and inclined to back off the leg

Good body awareness is paramount for these types of horses or for horses that are **blind in one eye**. Self-confidence and trust in the rider and handler will go a long way to helping them become more consistent in their day-to-day lives and performance.

Good body awareness is paramount for horses that are blind in one eye

The eye is a good indicator of how the horse feels and can give you information about his personality. A large, soft eye that can be easily seen when standing in front of the horse is usually indicative of a generous, uncomplicated horse although other facial features should also be taken into account.

A large soft eye is generally the sign of a generous and easy going temperament

A horse labelled 'sour' often has a **hard, almond-shaped eye**, but in truth a sour horse is more likely to be a sore horse. As tension is released through the body and potential causes for discomfort are removed, the eye will become softer in appearance and rounder in shape.

An almond-shaped eye may be a sign that the horse is uncomfortable

The eyelids can give you clues as to how your horse is feeling. Wrinkled lids can be a sign of concern and may be accompanied by stress dips and a tight or unevenly muscled forehead. Puffy lids may be linked to digestive disturbances and may alter as the diet changes or as anxiety levels diminish.

(Left) Puffy lids can be a sign of digestive disturbance

(Below) Stress dips, wrinkled lids and a tight forehead can be a sign of discomfort or concern

Ears and poll

The poll is an important part of the anatomy and can provide significant information on how the horse may function and behave. There is a close relationship between the poll, hyoid bones, TMJ, head and neck (see p.22).

Horses that are **ear shy** are often extremely tight through the poll and upper neck and may have a floppy lower lip (see p.54). Horses with tense polls may be prone to sudden reactive behaviour such as rearing. Such tension can also make the horse more prone to being startled and flinging up his head. If this occurs when the horse is standing under a low roof or stable doorway, the impact can result in further damage to the poll, exacerbating the problem. Tension in the poll may also cause tripping or stumbling because it is nearly always accompanied by restricted movement between the first two cervical vertebrae, C1 and C2 or the atlas and axis (see p.61), which affect movement of the front limbs.

Horses that are tight around the poll are often ear shy

With a horse that is tense in these areas the appearance of the ears may be altered with the horse looking as though he has **one ear set lower or further forward** than the other. Once such tension is reduced, the ears generally look more even.

This mare is tight through the poll and TMJ. The top of her neck is straight and she is over-developed around the poll...

... This makes it is hard for her to soften and lengthen through the neck and back and it is linked to unwanted behaviours such as rushing and napping

Tension around the poll will affect the appearance of the ears

Tight ears are often linked to tension in the forehead, the TMJ, poll and the upper part of the neck. Often circulation to the ear is inhibited and the tips may be cold to the touch. This is not always an indicator of the horse's general body temperature and is more consistent with horses that are ear shy. If tension is present around the base of the ear, the whole ear may appear tight and will generally lack subtlety in movement. The horse with this tension pattern is more prone to pinning back his ears as a means of expression and may appear to be generally intolerant. He may also have almond-shaped

eyes and tight, pinched nostrils, and will generally dislike contact. Reducing tension through the face, ears and neck and addressing any underlying causes for concern or discomfort will bring about dramatic changes.

Acupressure and the ears

There are many acupressure points in the ear linked to the overall health of the horse. Horses with imbalances in other parts of the body may have one specific spot on the ear that is persistently sensitive. There is a shock point located at the tip of each ear and horses that have suffered a trauma may be constantly cold in the tip of the ear. Working this point on a horse that is distressed or in extreme pain can literally save his life by preventing him from going into, or bringing him out of shock.

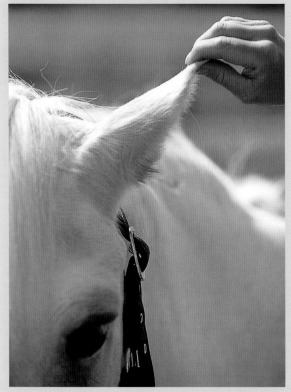

There is a shock point at the tip of the ear

As the ears are linked to vestibular balance (see p.15), horses that have tension around the ear may find it hard to move in self-carriage. They may tend to draw back slightly through the upper part of the neck or may work consistently above the vertical. In the stable they may stand with their head high and when in hand or under saddle may move forward if asked to lower their neck.

Tension through the poll also affects the horse's ability to maintain self-carriage and in some situations they may bolt

INDICATORS OF TENSION AROUND THE EARS AND POLL

Horses with tension around the ears and poll are also likely to:

- Dislike having their forelock touched
- Be concerned about movement over their heads
- Find it hard to walk under objects or low stable doors
- Pull back when tied
- Shoot off when the headcollar is being removed
- Be difficult to halter and bridle
- Be noise-sensitive
- Be difficult to catch
- Be concerned about having their lower legs touched

Neck

The neck is made up of seven cervical vertebrae. Like the back, it influences and is influenced by every part of the horse's body. The first two vertebrae, the atlas and the axis or C1 and C2, allow the head to nod up and down and to move from side to side. The other cervical vertebrae (C3–7) allow the neck to arch and bend.

Tension in the neck affects balance and body awareness. It can also influence a horse's wellbeing as there are important acupressure points on the neck that relate to digestion and health – the Stomach, Small Intestine, Large Intestine and Lung meridians are four of the meridians that pass through the neck. Chinese medicine holds that skin conditions can arise from problems with the Stomach, Lung or Liver meridians, and it is not uncommon to find tension through the neck in horses that suffer from skin allergies. Many modalities, including osteopathy, physiotherapy, chiropractic and cranial-sacral osteopathy, place great emphasis on the health and mobility of the spine for correct organ function, and problems with both the neck and back can give rise to a host of unwanted behaviours.

Alternative treatments for neck problems

Much can be done from the ground to reduce problems in the neck (see Free Up Your Horse, pp.76–146), however, sometimes other treatments may also be useful. An acupuncture point on the Small Intestine meridian, approximately one hand's width behind the jowl on both sides of the neck, is used for softening hard muscles and balancing the glands. Hormone imbalances can give rise to over-sensitivity and tension in this area, and even geldings may display hormonal behaviour, such as squealing and striking when touched around the poll and jowl.

Osteopathy, physiotherapy or appropriate gentle chiropractic work will help release the vertebrae. As the horse begins to free up in the upper part of the neck you may notice a discharge from one or both nostrils.

Conformation of the neck determines, to a certain degree, the suitability of a horse for a chosen discipline. However, while breed type determines its set and shape, **tension or restricted movement in the neck** have a direct influence on stride length, body awareness, the ability to move forward, proprioception, range of movement, and collection – and, therefore, how well the horse can perform. Gadgets that tie a horse down can create the illusion that he is working in a balanced and collected frame. However, inappropriate use of such gadgets from an early age can cause many problems for him throughout his adult life as they inhibit the natural movement of the back and hindquarters. The more restricted the horse

A tight neck will limit the horse's ability to engage his hindquarters

becomes in the upper part of his neck, the tighter he will be in the lumbar and pelvic area.

Because so much attention is paid to getting a horse working through from behind to improve hind limb action, the source of the problem may be overlooked: lack of engagement often stems from **a neck that is tight, contracted and unevenly muscled**. Some muscles may be over-bulky and others underdeveloped, or the cervical vertebrae may be over-defined. You may notice the mane 'jumping' as the horse lowers or raises his head – another indicator of tight muscles and ligaments. Changes in the way the mane lies generally correspond to tension in the neck, although it also changes direction where a swirl is present in the coat.

Tension in the neck affects a horse's ability to learn, alters his spatial awareness and can cause problems

Changes in the way the mane lies can be linked to areas of tension

with depth perception and changes in light. This can make it hard for horses moving from and into trailers, boxes and stables. Horses that are tight in the neck can be spooky and concerned over bright objects. They may react to something they have been past happily several times before as tension in the upper part of the neck can influence the optic nerve. They may be worse in the summer when more light is reflected off shiny surfaces such as white boards, cars and water.

Pulling back when tied up may be due to tension in the neck – the horse suddenly 'sees' the wall and startles even though they may have been standing quietly for a while. The action of pulling back causes more pressure and damage in the area and the cycle continues. **Pushy behaviour or crowding** when being handled can also be attributed to tension in some part of the neck and the horse may find it hard to stand since the neck is so important for balance. He may also have problems turning his head, raising or lowering his head, and arching or bending his neck. He may involuntarily nod or wobble his head from side to side when moving, and lead with his nose rather than flexing through the neck when turning left or right.

If tension has been present for a while, **volatile outbursts** may occur as the horse literally loses his head due to impaired blood flow to the brain. The horse may appear to be shut down and will often have a hard, almond-shaped eye, which changes completely once the underlying cause has been addressed. As tension affects the elasticity of the skin many horses that are tight in the

Tension in the upper part of the neck can trigger hormonal behaviour

neck find needles extremely uncomfortable and may explode when injected or blood samples are taken. Again, once tension in the neck has been released, this reaction usually changes completely.

The strong nuchal ligament supports the head and neck and allows the neck to be raised and lowered. If the horse has worked in a persistent **high-headed frame** he may struggle to lower his neck, even at rest, as movement in this ligament may have become limited. Horses that have been habitually in the high-headed posture for some time may feel insecure about lowering their head as it changes their balance so dramatically. Even if a lower head carriage can be achieved through leading work and groundwork, the horse may not be able to maintain this posture for more than a few moments initially and will generally keep reverting to a high head carriage. Exercises to release tension in the neck are obviously extremely beneficial, but working on achieving better balance all

round, through ground and ridden exercises, can help the horse learn to carry himself in a more effective and more relaxed way.

Tightness in the neck of a horse with a high head carriage is accompanied by a **hollow or dropped back**. There will be a dip in the top line in front of the withers and overdevelopment of muscles in the upper part of the neck. The fifth and sixth cervical vertebrae will be prominent and there may be rub marks from the reins in this area. The horse is usually 'fixed' through the base of the neck. To initiate forward movement he may raise his head before moving forward or fling up his head when asked for any transition. This will always affect his ability to engage behind and transitions will be awkward and ungainly. Such a horse will often find it hard to work in a straight line and may drift when working down the centre line.

If tension in the neck is accompanied by a **low head carriage,** the horse may have restricted movement through the throatlatch area and work consistently above or behind the vertical. He may curl his neck and work with his nose towards his chest. He is likely to be heavy in the hand as he needs to lean on the bit for support due to the inability to lengthen and soften his neck. He may be hard to get moving or difficult to stop.

Tension in the neck is often accompanied by hollowing behind the shoulder and in front of the wither

> ### INDICATORS OF A TENSE NECK
>
> Horses that are tight in the neck may also:
>
> - Nap
> - Find it hard to move forward from the leg
> - Spin in hand and under saddle
> - Rush
> - Work on the forehand
> - Drop behind or come above the bit when asked for collection
> - Bite
> - Dislike having their mane pulled
> - Be concerned about being handled from both sides

Shoulders and chest

The conformation of the shoulders determines stride length, with the angle being similar to that of the hoof and the pastern. Tension and restricted movement in the shoulders will create balance problems and are usually accompanied by tension in the neck, back and hindquarters. The foot balance should also be checked.

Tight or unevenly muscled shoulders limit stride length...

Stiff shoulders are usually accompanied by tension through the neck and back. This mare has a stiff, straight neck with typical mane changes in front of the shoulders

A horse that is **tight in the shoulders** may balance or lean on the handler and the riders' hands since he finds it hard to work in a balanced frame. The gait will be uneven and the horse may be 'girthy', as tension in the shoulder is often accompanied by sensitivity around the girth area. Some horses with tension around the girth area may buck when asked to move forward or when mounted. The horse with this tension pattern may be stiff through the whole body and lack impulsion from behind since the shoulders must be free to allow hind limb engagement. He may stand base narrow, with the front feet close together, and may hold his elbows close to his ribcage or stand habitually with one forelimb forward or out to the side

...and the horse may lean on the rider's hands for support

Horses with **tension through the chest and shoulders** may be inclined to strike or paw the ground when concerned. Tension in this area can be as a result of an uneven rider, a fall, rough play with another horse, lack of education, poor saddle fit, poor conformation or birth trauma. The horse may develop unevenly through the shoulders and chest and the conformation of the front limbs and hooves may vary, with the feet being different shapes or one knee or shoulder looking higher than the other. He may find it hard to lift through the withers and may develop tight muscles in front of or behind the shoulder blade. There may be thickening over the top of the scapula. Under saddle the horse may continually throw the rider forward and to one side, thus exacerbating the problem.

Horses often use the part of the body that is carrying tension to express themselves. Those that are tight through the shoulders may be inclined to paw or strike

Cervico-thoracal Syndrome

Rikki Schultz is a veterinary surgeon based in Denmark. She uses TTEAM, chiropractic work and acupuncture and treats many horses suffering from what she describes as Cervico-thoracal Syndrome. She believes this can occur as a result of an injury, such as a kick to the chest by another horse, or from other damage such as, for example, the horse running into a fence post or flipping over backwards. It involves rotation of the lower cervical vertebra (C7) and the first thoracic vertebra (T1), which has a knock-on effect through the rest of the body. Rikki has successfully treated many horses that suffer from some of the symptoms associated with this condition and would like more research done in the area. She believes that the condition may also originate from birth trauma in some instances with the foal developing a club, or more upright, foot on one side as it matures. It is certainly food for thought and gives other possibilities for correct diagnosis and treatment of horses with otherwise inexplicable front limb lameness.

Hollowing behind the shoulders is often accompanied by a dip in the neck muscles in front of the wither and raised, hardened areas on the top of the shoulder blade. Contrary to popular opinion, this is not just due to conformation, nor is it breed specific, as in the thoroughbred, but is linked to improper muscle development through poor saddle fit, injury, dental issues or inappropriate training. If allowed to develop properly by addressing the underlying cause these areas often fill out very quickly and a top line is achieved.

Due to a poorly fitting saddle, this horse has developed raised areas over the top of the shoulder and works persistently in a high-headed frame and on the forehand. This photograph clearly shows the resulting over-developed areas and those where there is a lack of muscle

As the horse develops behind the shoulders, the chest will follow suit. Conformation obviously plays a part in determining the general frame of the horse but the chest is a good indicator of how the horse is working through the shoulders and first part of the back. **A narrow chest or uneven and over-developed chest musculature** often accompanies lack of muscle behind the shoulder or restricted movement through the base of the neck and shoulders.

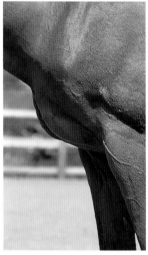

An over-developed chest can be a sign of a horse that works on the forehand

This horse is more developed on the left side of the chest

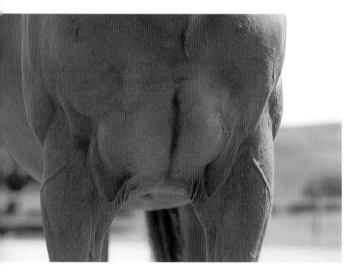

The chest muscles will tell you how even the stride is and how the weight is distributed through the front and hind limbs. This horse is more developed on the right side

INDICATORS OF CHEST AND SHOULDER PROBLEMS

Horses with tense or unevenly developed shoulders and chest are likely to:

- Trip or stumble
- Have a short, choppy and/or uneven stride
- Be spooky
- Lean on the bit
- Be difficult to rug and/or saddle up
- Fall in through the shoulder through turns and circles
- Find it hard to strike off on a particular rein
- Leave a front limb behind when jumping
- Struggle to travel and/or load
- Find it hard to bring the front limb forward for the farrier
- Throw up the head in upward and downward transitions
- Be reactive to movement
- Poke the nose when ridden
- Nod their head
- Headshake

Withers, back and hindquarters

The back consists of 18 thoracic vertebrae, six lumbar vertebrae, and the sacrum. Correct muscle development, saddle fit, rug fit, rider posture, and training are vital to minimize the risk of injury and for the overall wellbeing and comfort of the horse. Other areas to check are the teeth, jaw, neck, shoulders, ribs, limbs and abdomen.

Horses that are **tight in the back** generally find it easier to behave in one extreme or another – either rushing and bolting or being sluggish and shut down. They may appear lazy and stuffy under saddle or may over-react to the rider's leg. They will often find it hard to truly settle and relax and can be sensitive through the ribs and belly and dislike being groomed. Any reactive behaviour while being saddled or rugged, such as moving away, kicking, pulling faces, going into freeze, grinding teeth or blowing out the belly, is generally indicative of discomfort or tension through the back. Horses with back problems may also become agoraphobic, box walk, walk fence lines, and be highly defensive about horses and people approaching from the side or behind. They may stand with their limbs underneath them or strung out, stand base narrow or base wide (see p.40) and will generally find it hard to stand square.

Back problems can often be found in horses that **dislike standing still**, whether they are tied, in-hand or under saddle. When being mounted, they may swing away or move off the minute the rider's foot is in the stirrup. Under saddle such horses often jig, arch their backs and may be spooky. They may start rushing once turned for home. Such horses often drift and trail their quarters when working in the school, and their movement may be mechanical rather than natural and free. Inability to track up and/or wobbly movement behind can be indicative of tension through the back as well as the neck. The horse will often be close behind or move with one hind limb working more towards the midline; this is generally accompanied by loss of articulation through the hock joint or other joints in the hind limb, often mirrored in the diagonal front limb. This pattern is usually linked to tension in the hip area and the horse may find it impossible to stand square.

Horses that are tight through the back will find it **hard to stretch down** and lengthen through the neck and back or to walk in balance on a loose rein. They also find it hard to round over jumps and may jump fast and flat, rushing before and after the fence. They may trail a limb, jump to one side, twist their body over the fence or buck as they land. They will struggle when worked in a confined space and through tight turns and circles. If asked to walk over raised poles in-hand or under saddle the horse may raise his head when lifting a front limb, rather than lowering his head, since tension in the back prevents the back from lifting, lengthening and releasing.

Tension through the back can change body awareness and many horses that are tight through the thoracic area are often **disconnected through the hindquarters**. They may panic if their hind limbs touch a pole, when working in-hand or under saddle. Similarly, they may struggle if asked to halt with the front limbs in front of a pole and their hind legs behind it, and may become extremely concerned.

Horses that are tight through the back tend to do things in one extreme or another, either rushing or being sluggish and shut down...

...They appear lazy and stuffy under saddle...

...or hollow and over-react to the rider's leg

Many horses that lack confidence are **tight in the upper part of thoracic spine.** They generally have shallow breathing and may be prone to frequent light sighing. They may buckle or lie down when being saddled and will

Twisting over a jump is a sign that the horse is unable to lift and curve his back

have a tendency to be habitually in the flight/fight reflex (see p.18). Since nothing occurs in isolation, the pelvis will often drop or tilt to one side to compensate for the tension in the first part of the back.

Tension in the lumbar area is often found in horses that frequently buck, particularly when asked for canter.

There may also be sensitivity in the flank, barrel and belly, and the horse may lose weight easily, or have the appearance of a saggy or bloated belly as a result of weak abdominal muscles. Lumbar tension often gives rise to the 'jumper's bump', as changes in the area and loss of muscle tone over the sacroiliac make the bony structures more prominent. This is accentuated through general loss of muscle tone over the hindquarters. If the horse is croup high, either through conformation or during a growth period, tension in the lumbar area and first part of the thoracic spine and shoulders will usually be present. The horse may swing out his hind limbs particularly when walking down hill and will generally find it hard to work in balance.

Issues around the **stifle joint,** apart from actual trauma to the stifle area itself, can sometimes arise as a result of tension in the horse's back. Tension or weakness in the loins may make the horse sensitive to contact around the sheath or frequently lower his penis when working.

Tension in the back can arise from a variety of issues. **Poor saddle fit** is often implicated, but it is important to be aware that tension in the back can occur as a knock-on effect from problems with the jaw, neck and feet, and these can give rise to the appearance of poor saddle fit, or they may alter the fit through loss of top line and muscle atrophy around the shoulders and in the back. **Rider posture** is also important since the rider can inadvertently cause uneven muscle development in the back, which influences every other part of the horse.

Lifting the head when working over raised poles may be a sign of tension through the back

A saggy or bloated belly is usually linked to a weak or non-existent top line

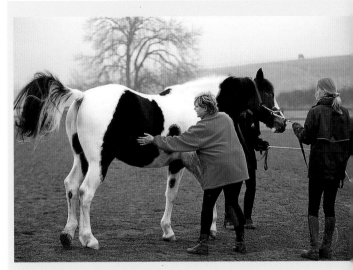

Sensitivity around the barrel...

INDICATORS OF TENSION IN HINDQUARTERS AND BACK

Tension in the hindquarters and back can also be linked to:

- Noise sensitivity
- Nervousness
- Concern about things moving behind the horse
- Difficulty in loading and travelling
- Bolting
- Kicking
- Issues with tail bandages
- Concern over leg wraps on the hind limbs
- Rushing through narrow spaces such as gateways
- Concern about personal space with horses and people
- Hormonal changes in mares
- Concerns about being shod or trimmed
- Trailing and scuffing hind feet
- Being disunited
- A tight tail or floppy tail

...is generally connected to sensitivity in the back

Ribs, belly and flanks

Sensitivity or blocked awareness through the ribs, belly or flank is most commonly linked to tension in the back and loin area, but can also be linked to uneven development through the chest and stiffness through the ribs. Other contributory factors can be diet, and digestive disturbance.

Horses with **tension or sensitivity in the belly** may be picky or fussy eaters, may bolt food or become aggressive when eating. They can be extremely sensitive to being groomed and may bite when touched on the ribs, belly or flank. Tension around the flank and belly can make it uncomfortable for brood mares to let their foals feed and cause stallions and geldings to have issues about having their sheath cleaned.

Horses that have tension through the barrel, belly and flank can be 'girthy' and either sluggish or over-reactive to the rider's leg. They may be ticklish around the stifle, be concerned about having their hind legs touched, liable to cow-kick and find it hard to pick up the hind leg for the farrier or to have the foot picked out.

Tension in the belly can also be linked to anxiety and worry. Since digestive function influences and is influenced by the mouth, horses with tension in the belly may have thick, sticky, white saliva or an excessively dry mouth. They may be in a permanent state of alert, lick their lips constantly or grind their teeth when concerned.

INDICATORS OF TENSION IN RIBS, BELLY OR FLANK

Horses with sensitivity in these areas may also:

- Be aggressive
- Lack engagement
- Have light shallow breathing
- Find it hard to relax
- Be concerned about horses or people approaching from the side
- Be prone to colic
- Have a tight or saggy, bloated abdomen
- Have puffy eyelids
- Be clingy to other horses

Tail

There are usually between 18 and 21 vertebrae in the tail. The tail is influenced by the back and hindquarters and is also linked to the mouth: if the horse is particularly tense around the mouth, the tail will often be tight as well. If the horse dislikes having his tail touched, work to release tension around the muzzle and chin can go a long way to helping nervous horses become more confident about having their tail handled. Similarly, if the horse habitually bites or nips and is reluctant to be handled around the muzzle, exercises to release tension in the tail can help the horse become less reactive to being touched and the mouthy behaviour often subsides.

Aside from this correlation, you can obtain a great deal of information about the horse from studying the tail. In the majority of cases, the tail will mirror the spine. The top of the tail can be likened to the shoulders and the end of the tailbone to the hindquarters. Horses that work on the forehand or are tight through the chest and shoulders are often clamped at the top of the dock and those with tension through the hindquarters and problems with engagement often have a corresponding stiffness at the end of the tailbone.

Horses that find it consistently **hard to release the tail** often have ongoing problems with the back; in the case of spinal problems such as kissing spine or stress fractures, it may be that the horse never really releases his tail. Lack of suppleness through the whole body and difficulties with lateral work usually result in a rigid, stick-like tail, while a floppy tail usually indicates complete disconnection and blocked awareness through the hindquarters and limbs.

The tail will also tend to be carried towards the tighter side of the horse or to the lower hip, and tail swishing is generally indicative of tension through the whole back or of concern.

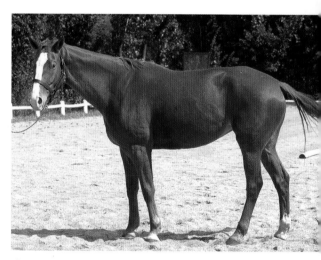

This mare is stiff through her neck and back, and her tail follows the same pattern

A kink in the tail will link to tension around the spine, and the tail will be carried to the lower or tighter side of the horse

Although tail swishing can be a sign of concern, it is also common in horses that are tight through the back

Legs

Tension through the shoulder and hindquarters will change flexibility through the entire leg and vice versa. Loss of articulation in the hock joint will influence and be influenced by the hip and/or back foot, while knee problems will influence and be influenced by tension in the shoulders and/or fore foot.

Cold lower legs are indicative of horses that are spooky and flight oriented. Objects moving on the ground, such as leaves or flapping plastic, will cause concern to the horse with inhibited circulation in the lower leg. The horse may struggle with polework and may panic if he

The movement and balance of the fore and hind limbs will affect and be affected by the shoulders, hips and feet

INDICATORS OF TENSION IN THE TAIL

Horses with tension in the tail are also likely to:

- Kick
- Find it hard to engage behind
- Be concerned about movement behind them
- Mouth or bite
- Rush
- Be either hard to get moving or hard to slow down
- Startle easily

This horse is weak through the loins and carries tension through the hips which influences how he stands and moves

touches the poles with his feet. Horses that drag their toes lack impulsion and are likely to have tension in the hindquarters and/or shoulders or blocked awareness through the back.

Tension in the elbow limits stride length. Even if the horse is 'tied in' at the elbow, regular bodywork can help achieve and maintain an increase in movement of the front limb. Tight fetlocks are also linked to tension in the neck and/or back, and simple gentle rocking of the fetlock joint when doing leg circles can go a long way to releasing problems further up the limb.

Optimal performance depends on conformation of the front limbs to a certain degree. It is, therefore, important that the front limbs are able to work effectively – although it has to be said that some horses with poor conformation have gone on to be high achievers. Conformational faults such as a twisted limb will alter the distribution of weight through the hooves but even if your horse has a conformational fault there are still plenty of things that you can do to minimize the effect his natural tendencies have upon his body.

INDICATORS OF LEG PROBLEMS

Horses with concerns over their legs may also:

- Have issues about having their legs handled

- Dislike having their legs washed off

- Have an increase in susceptibility to mud fever

- Be concerned about walking through water or over different surfaces

- Have travelling and loading issues

- Trip and stumble

- Struggle with the farrier

Ting points

Around each coronary band there are acupressure points that correspond to the twelve major meridians in the body. Called ting points, these are the beginning or ending point of a meridian. If there is an imbalance in the meridians, the coronary band may have areas of puffiness, softness, raised hair, dry skin or indentation. Traditional Chinese medicine is a relatively complex approach, so it is not simply a case of working out which ting point is indicating an imbalance since the origin of the problem may well be elsewhere in the meridian system. However, you can use this knowledge to recognize that your horse may have a problem or to note if anything changes and find relevant professional help.

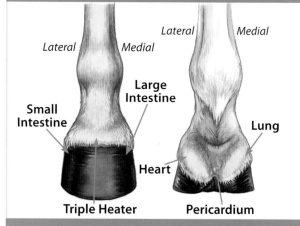

Ting Points Fore Leg

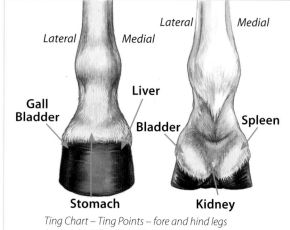

Ting Points Hind Leg

Ting Chart – Ting Points – fore and hind legs (copyright Tallgrass Publishing)

Hooves

The hoof acts as a shock absorber and is the foundation for every other joint in the body. Hoof care is vital for the overall wellbeing of the horse: the old adage 'no foot, no horse' is true.

As with all tension patterns, nothing exists in isolation. Tension in the neck, shoulder and back influences the angle of the front limb; poor muscle development or tension behind the shoulder, for example, can contribute to tight elbows, which causes the distribution of weight to fall laterally through the front limb and hoof. Problems in the lumbar area and hindquarters can alter the balance through the hind limbs; for example, tension in the loins and pelvis can give rise to a cow-hocked stance, which affects the balance of the back feet. If problems exist within the balance of the hoof, the gait and wellbeing of the horse are affected as the foot provides support for every other joint in the body.

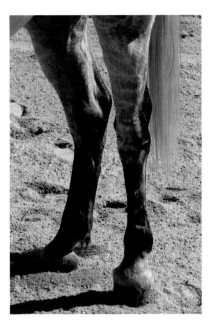

Damage to the hind limb has altered the hoof growth. Understandably, this horse is reactive under saddle and carries a significant amount of tension through the hindquarters

Tight shoulders affect the angle of the front limbs. Such conformation can be changed with appropriate bodywork and groundwork

(Below) Tight hips and a pelvis that is tipped forward will affect the weight distribution through the hooves and therefore the way they develop and grow

Movement is crucial for the health of the foot, since it encourages blood flow to the hoof. Horses that are stabled for the majority of their lives or have restricted movement through the limbs may be more prone to diseases of the foot, and poor foot care can cause a variety of problems, including thrush and other fungal conditions.

INDICATORS OF FOOT PROBLEMS

Horses that have pain or imbalance in the foot may:

- Be labelled as stubborn or sour
- Not want to move forward freely
- Refuse to jump
- Find it hard to pick up one leg as this places greater strain on a sore foot
- Have changes in the height of the coronary band around the top of the hoof
- Have blisters or rough edges around the coronary band
- Wear the hoof or shoe unevenly
- Have heat in the foot
- Develop corns
- Show concern about shoes being nailed on
- Stand unevenly – pointing a foot or rocking backwards to take the weight off the front feet
- Be reactive to having the lower limb handled

Stay positive

Now that you have made a thorough assessment of your horse, do not panic if you note unevenness through his body. Remind yourself that no horse is symmetrical. If you follow the suggestions in the next section, even horses with very complicated tension patterns generally change dramatically within two weeks, unless there are underlying problems. If problems persist you must call your vet to do an examination, but make a checklist to chart the progress of your horse and answer the following questions:

- Have you been able to work through the suggestions in this book?
- Have you been able to link the behaviour or reduced performance to over- or underdeveloped areas on the horse's body?
- Are there or were there possible contributory factors, such as saddle fit, oral or foot imbalance?
- Can these be/have these been changed?
- Are there changes and improvements, however small, in the horse's behaviour and performance?
- Have other problems become apparent that may have contributed to the problem?
- Is the reactive or unwanted behaviour diminishing?
- Has the horse generally improved and settled through the work?
- Are there still small consistent improvements?
- Can you establish a pattern of behaviour, ie, can you pinpoint when problems occur?
- Does the horse now move freely when loose and only changes when ridden?

If the answer to these questions is 'yes' you are probably on the right path.

Angel – Part One

Angel is a young dark bay mare I met while working with horses belonging to the Sa[...] Land in Cyprus. I had flown there with TTEAM Practitioners Tina Constance and Mar[...] TTEAM workshops for the three Saddle Clubs at Episkopi, Dhekalia and Akrotiri and ha[...] Angel on our second day. She was not the horse you would choose to work with in an uns[...] off, for a whole day in temperatures reaching 30 degrees Celsius, but given the extent of he[...] at the Akrotiri Saddle Club for one day, I had no choice. Suffice to say 'angel' was not the wo[...] when I first saw this little mare in action – 'devil's spawn' might have been nearer the mark.

Angel was born in April 2000 and was bought by the Akrotiri Saddle Club the following Septem[...] not been handled at all and had allegedly been beaten by a man; not surprisingly, she reared when a foal s[...]p was put on her in preparation for her journey to the club, and fell over backwards, injuring herself on the poll by her right ear. She then had to be sedated to be loaded into the lorry. On her arrival at Akrotiri, she was put into a paddock on her own and her wound was treated. The ointment used came into contact with her eye, triggering a reaction that required frequent veterinary assistance. After everything had finally healed, Angel was left unhandled for a few months but then sustained an injury to her stifle that again required veterinary help. She reacted badly to the treatment and nearly died. The wound did not heal very well and Angel was subjected to many vet's visits until the autumn of 2001. By then, understandably, the human race was not rating highly in her eyes, she had developed some dangerous habits and these had escalated to the point where no-one wanted to handle her.

The problem was made worse because Angel had had no contact with other horses. I confess my heart sinks when I am asked to work with horses that are becoming dangerous to handle and that have been raised alone. Horses raised without equine company of a similar age often lack boundaries and have never discovered that excessive rough behaviour is unacceptable. They do not know how to be a part of a group and can appear pushy and controlling towards people and other horses as they mature. Angel was no exception. Her lack of socialization and her many negative experiences with humans, particularly men, had resulted in a reactive and defensive mare. At the age of two, she was so difficult that her owners were considering euthanasia.

Hilary Gibbins purchased Angel in the spring of 2002 and slowly began to work with her in hand to try to establish some degree of trust. Although Angel responded well to Hilary, she was extremely reactive to other people, including Hilary's husband Andy, but Hilary persevered. She even backed the mare on her own and would take her out for short rides, but Angel's day-to-day behaviour remained the same. Hilary was forced to continue to keep her on her own because she bullied any horse that Hilary tried to integrate into her life. A new male groom on the yard triggered problems. He was understandably frightened of the mare, and would wave a bucket at her to keep her at bay while he was cleaning her pen; naturally, this made her behaviour even worse. Eventually, the decision was made to stop all staff entering Angel's pen for anything other than cleaning, and her food was tipped over the fence.

As there was no-one else who could look after the little mare, Hilary's life began to be taken over by Angel. Because she had to check Angel three times a day, she couldn't go anywhere. The mare chased anyone entering her pen, and even began to turn on Hilary at feed times. When the vet came to give her annual inoculation, Angel exploded, attacking him with her front feet, teeth and hind legs. He was forced to leave without injecting her. Angel became increasingly difficult to catch and seemed to be extremely jealous of Andy. He couldn't approach the mare without Angel screaming, pinning her ears and swinging her quarters around in an attempt to double barrel him. Hilary became more and more demoralized and began to feel that perhaps everyone was right and that Angel should be destroyed, especially as she herself would be leaving the island the following year. No-one else would be prepared to take on this very reactive, highly defensive horse. Luckily for Angel, however, Hilary wasn't prepared to give up just yet. She re-assessed how she was handling the mare and decided to spend time just sitting on the fence being with her and, in this way, slowly rebuilt some of the trust that had been lost between her and Angel. (Concluded on pp.96–97.)

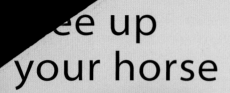

...ee up
your horse

You can't change the past but you can shape the future

You can help your horse gain freedom of movement through simple and effective exercises that can be easily slotted into your usual routine. The exercises in this section are divided into bodywork, groundwork and ridden work (see pp.79–80). They can be adapted to suit the individual horse, and spending even a few minutes a day can bring about dramatic changes to the way he performs and behaves. They can also improve the balance and co-ordination of the handler and rider.

Training

Training at any stage should enhance and promote the physical, mental and emotional wellbeing, development, attitude and aptitude of every horse, regardless of its age or job. Sadly, this is not always the case, and some disciplines and training systems freely acknowledge that a number of horses will be ruined in the pursuit of learning. Sacrificing one horse to achieve success with another is simply not necessary. Good foundations, awareness and a flexible and adaptable schedule that allows the horse to learn and develop without the use of fear and force will vastly increase the chances of producing a confident equine that is happy, sound and consistent in his work well into old age.

Selecting a trainer or training method

Picking the right trainer and training method for your horse is as important as all other aspects of horse care. Ask yourself the following questions to see whether a particular approach is appropriate for you:

■ Is what the trainer says and what the trainer does the same?

■ If you could put yourself in the horse's hooves how would you feel, and what would you be learning from the experience?

■ How do you truly feel in your gut and in your heart when you watch the trainer working with or handling the horse?

■ Could you do the same?

■ What does the trainer do when what they are doing or asking the horse to do doesn't work? Do they have alternative ideas and try another approach, do they make the lesson easier for the horse to understand, do they give the horse a break or do they do more of the same but harder?

■ If you are watching the trainer on a video or DVD, try turning the sound down; if you are at a demonstration cover your ears. It can be quite enlightening to watch the horse's expressions and responses without being distracted by words and sounds.

TTEAM and Connected Riding

Two major inspirations in my work are TTEAM and Connected Riding (see p.5). The exercises you will find here are based on these methods and require very little in the way of special equipment. TTEAM uses some specific equipment including a flat lead line, a long white dressage schooling stick, referred to as a wand, and lengths of coloured rope, 6.5m (21ft) long. If you can't find TTEAM lead lines, soft climbing rope (4.25m/14ft) long is a good alternative. In addition, sheepskin buffs or soft rubber groomers are used for work with horses that are sensitive to hand contact. Two other important pieces of equipment are the neck ring, an adjustable hoop made from stiffened lariat rope, and the balance rein, a 1.8m (6ft) long adjustable strap made from rope and leather and fastened with a buckle. Both are used to improve balance (see pp.128 and 119).

TTEAM uses a specific lead line and a long white dressage stick, referred to as a wand

Peggy Cummings has designed a headcollar for her in-hand exercises, which can be fitted to the horse's head more snugly than a traditional headcollar. A headcollar with an adjustable noseband is also effective. Connected Riding also uses the wand, TTEAM lead lines and shorter lengths of rope for the in-hand exercises.

Peggy Cummings has designed her own headcollars and uses lengths of coloured rope for groundwork exercises

Bodywork

Bodywork is used to release tension, reduce stiffness, improve circulation, increase body awareness and improve mobility and performance. It can enable horses to overcome a fear of contact, change an expectation or memory of pain, and helps horses to be easier to handle and train. Bodywork also helps to trigger the parasympathetic nervous system (see p.13), encourages deep and rhythmical breathing, which boosts the immune system, improves sensory integration, reduces stress, improves performance and promotes a sense of wellbeing in the horse.

Bodywork releases tension...

TTouches

The various TTouches that make up part of the TTEAM technique break down into three groups: circles, slides and lifts. The simple circular TTouches often have a dramatic effect on horses and can elicit profound changes in a short space of time. They can be done anywhere on the horse's body and can teach a horse to accept and enjoy contact. The slides are light and calming and are used on the body, mane or tail. They are also used to link the other touches together, to initiate contact or to relax the horse. The lifts move the actual skin. They increase circulation and release tension and muscular spasms. In this section TTouches are used on pp.94–95, 102, 130 and 143. The majority of the TTouches and leading exercises are named after animals to create images that will help you remember the movements.

...and promotes a sense of relaxation while building trust between the horse and the handler

Groundwork

Groundwork develops flexibility and balance and helps to establish a solid foundation for ridden work, as the horse learns true self-carriage. It enables him to learn how to move his body in a more effective way without placing unnecessary stress on one particular joint or joints, releases tension, teaches focus and obedience and improves co-ordination. Groundwork enables the horse to become active rather than simply reactive.

Ridden work

Ridden exercises build on the lessons taught from the ground and help to establish free, balanced movement under saddle. They range from bodywork on the horse under saddle to release tension and increase awareness, ridden exercises, including polework, to aid correct carriage and muscle development, and the use of simple equipment such as the TTEAM balance rein and neck ring.

Groundwork helps to develop flexibility and improves mind–body awareness

(Below) Ridden exercises improve balance and co-ordination

Balance

All the exercises that follow will help improve the horse's posture and therefore his balance. When a horse is out of balance he will tend to do things at speed, so the slow precise groundwork movements of TTEAM and Connected Riding play a pivotal role. They work on physical, vestibular and visual balance by encouraging the horse to release and lengthen his neck and back. This in turn helps with proprioception and body awareness, reduces noise sensitivity and encourages more efficient use of the brain and body as movement becomes more considered.

It is said that a horse only has so many circles in him. Working purely on the lunge or in a lunging pen can put uneven strain on the joints and can inadvertently teach a horse to work with his neck and head turned to the outside and to brace through the inside shoulder. Incorporating other aspects of groundwork into the routine, or lunging the horse around a square pattern of poles, develops balance, suppleness and straightness. By being creative you encourage the horse to focus on the exercises thus increasing his concentration span and ability to learn.

Using poles adds variety to in-hand work and helps to keep the horse mentally stimulated

Other exercises are more specific in what they teach. For example, the teeter totter (a low level seesaw), helps a horse learn how to adjust his balance and can be practised both in hand and under saddle. It can assist with loading problems and lack of confidence and helps the handler to become clear and precise with their signals. With practice the horse can learn how to tip the teeter totter up and down when standing on the balance point of the seesaw by simply moving his centre of gravity but not his feet.

This low-level see-saw helps to improve balance and is a wonderful way of teaching horses to travel quietly and safely in a horse box or float

Points to consider

- Although these exercises are simple, the techniques take practice to refine. Some require a certain amount of physical effort. If you are suffering from back, knee, hip, wrists or shoulder problems you may be unable to carry out certain exercises such as the leg circles. If at any point you feel uncomfortable – STOP. You don't need to do every exercise in each section in order to make a difference to your horse.

- If your horse 'won't' do any of the exercises it is likely that he actually 'can't'. This may be because he doesn't understand what is being asked of him or because it is difficult for him to release the tension and connect to a specific part of his body. Be patient, be clear in what you are asking him to do and give him time to process the information. He has to hear or feel the signal, think about the signal, then move his body accordingly. If he continues to struggle, break the exercise down into smaller steps or try something different.

- Remember to keep checking your posture. Horses continually change their balance to compensate for outside influences. For every action there is an equal and opposite reaction and if you try to push a horse, he will simply push you back in order to re-balance. You won't be leaning on your horse while doing the exercises, but you might inadvertently be encouraging him to move his body in a less than functional manner by bracing in your own body or by leaning on the headcollar, lead line or reins. With awareness you can use your posture and balance to help the horse, and speed up the effectiveness of the work.

- When doing the bodywork and leading exercises look for signs that the horse is beginning to release and connect. Positive changes include a softening of the eye, a release and lengthening through the neck and back, draining of the nostrils, lowering of the head and/or a more even posture both in movement and in halt.

When working, look for signs that the horse is beginning to release and connect

Otto – Part Two

Otto with Tony and Sarah

Exercises for the rider

Free up your horse

Before starting on the exercises for your...
Cummings places great emphasis on your...
of the posture of the rider and...
flexibility, co-ordinate...
awareness in the...
with...
...e us
...mulate a
...ramme that could
...dapted as required.

The final pieces to the jigsaw came in the shape of a wonderful McTimoney therapist, a top class farrier, and an excellent equine dental technician, Lucinda Stockley, who could maintain Otto's teeth on a regular basis, as the damaged pelvis affected his entire posture, resulting in uneven dental wear. Lucinda is also a TTEAM practitioner, an excellent rider and worked with me for many years. As he grew stronger and more stable behind, she began to compete Otto in showing classes, working hunter classes and dressage. In his first showing competition he was placed second in a Horse of the Year Show qualifier. With his wonderful temperament and impeccable manners Otto went on to be placed in the top three in virtually every outing at local, county and national level even taking Reserve Ridden Champion in one show.

Otto has taken part in several photoshoots and participates in all the TTEAM clinics here at Tilley Farm. He is a kind and wonderful teacher for people of all skill levels. He even appeared in season seven of Buffy the Vampire Slayer ridden by Tony and has a small fan club of people who keep him supplied with mints.

This horse is a real testimony to TTEAM and all the other people that have helped him. Despite his injury, Otto has gone on to achieve some remarkable results and proves that function can still be attained even though the physical form may be somewhat impaired. Judges would always compliment Lucinda for the free moving, balanced ride that Otto gave them. Not bad for a horse that is two inches higher on one side of his pelvis than the other.

...horse,
...urself. Peggy
...on the importance
...handler in encouraging
...ion and increased body
...e horse. By working on your own
...u can develop core strength and balance
...ut tensing or putting undue stress or strain on
individual joints, ligaments or tendons. The result
will be a longer, healthier and happier working life, a
greater sense of wellbeing, less fatigue, a better riding
posture and, of course, a more contented horse.

Feldenkrais arm exercise

This variation of a Feldenkrais exercise is an extremely
effective way of increasing the range of movement
through your upper body. It only takes a few minutes and
is an excellent way of relieving any tension or bracing in
your body before you start working with your horse.

- Stand with your feet
  shoulder width apart
  and with your weight
  distributed as evenly as
  possible through both
  legs and feet. Raise your
  right arm in front of you,
  so that it is parallel to the
  ground.

- Now take your arm back
  as far as is comfortable.
  Note how far you can
  take it by looking where
  the tips of your fingers
  are pointing, such as
  towards a mark on the
  wall, a landmark, or fence
  post.

- Lower your arm and keeping your feet in the same
  position turn back to face forwards again.

- Raise your right arm in
  front of your body so that
  your fingers are pointing
  directly ahead of you.
  Keep your head and
  neck straight so that you
  remain looking ahead
  and take your arm slowly
  out to the side so that
  your arm stops in line
  with the slope of your
  shoulder.

- Move your arm forward again and then take it back out
  to the side. Repeat this movement five times in total.
  Lower your arm for a moment.

- Raise your arm in front
  of you as before but this
  time turn your neck and
  head slightly to the left
  each time you take your
  arm out to the right side.
  Again keep your arm in
  line with the slope of your
  shoulder. Some people
  find this very difficult, as
  it is more habitual to turn
  the head in the same
  direction of the arm.

- As you bring your arm back in front of you, turn your
  neck and head to face the front so that you are looking
  forwards as your fingers point straight ahead.

- Repeat this five times in total. At no point should you
  feel any pull or tension in your shoulder, neck or back.
  If raising your arm is uncomfortable just raise it slightly.
  The exercise will still work.

- Lower your arm and keeping your feet in the same position go back to the beginning of this exercise and see how far you can take your arm behind you now. See how near the original mark your fingers are now. Most people find their range of movement has vastly increased. Some even find it has doubled.

- Repeat the exercise with the left arm or for fun try a slight variation. Check to see how far you can take your left arm as before but this time, instead of doing the non-habitual movements, let your arm rest by your side and picture yourself going through the motions. Think through the two different exercises five times and then see how near you are to your original point. Some people are stunned to discover that the range of movement has increased just as much as when they were actually moving the other arm. Imagine what we could achieve if we could apply this to our riding and to our horses. We could all reach Grand Prix levels from the comfort of our sofa.

Walking over poles

This is a quick exercise to unlock the pelvis and hips and to improve balance. Lay a pole on the ground and walk along the length of the pole criss-crossing your legs over it. Experiment by moving at different speeds and see how it affects your balance.

Wrist bands

Keeping the wrists straight, with the thumbs on top, when riding is important as it maintains a light and consistent contact with the horse's mouth and enables the rider to be extremely subtle with the rein aids. Even the best riders develop habits that they aren't aware of until someone is there to point them out.

If you have a persistent problem maintaining the correct hand position it might stem from a disconnection elsewhere in your posture. Wearing sports wrist bands, which are cheap and easy to obtain, can be extremely beneficial. By bringing awareness to your wrists and hands, they trigger the brain to pay attention to that part of the body and will help you to become more connected through your hands.

Bending the wrists and losing the connection with the horse's mouth via the reins is a common habit

Use wrist bands to draw your attention to the position of your wrists and hands

Free up your horse

Body wraps

Body wraps work on the same principle of increasing awareness. Use stretchy exercise bandages or elastic tail bandages on your upper body to feel how you position yourself on the horse. As your shoulders and elbows will be compensating for the position of your pelvis and lower leg, and vice versa, body wrapping the upper body in a variety of ways can improve your overall balance. You should become more aware of how you sit and move on a horse and can alter your posture accordingly.

Body wraps on the upper body can help the rider become more...

...aware of any tendencies to sit to one side, drop a shoulder or hollow or arch the back and so on

Neutral pelvis

Like horses, many people are consistently in front of or behind the vertical and develop habitual patterns of bracing to compensate for an uneven posture. Core muscles maintain the human body's ability to be upright. When the rider is in neutral pelvis the core muscles engage automatically, which helps them to maintain balance on a horse in any situation including spooking, napping and sudden freezing. As resistance only comes from resistance, horses are less likely to disconnect, evade

Some people ride in front of the vertical...

...and others ride behind the vertical. Both positions inadvertently push the horse onto the forehand

the aids or brace in their body when the rider is in true balance. Neutral pelvis is a Connected Riding exercise that enables the horse to move freely through his body and enables the rider to be a pro-active part of the ridden process. It helps the rider to become a part of the solution instead of inadvertently being a part of the problem and can be easily achieved by the majority of riders, regardless of their age or experience.

- First find neutral pelvis when sitting on a chair and then use the same principles in the saddle.

- Sit near the edge of the chair and walk forward a fraction on your seat bones. Sit with your feet and knees apart. Rest your hands on your thighs or allow them to hang loosely by your sides. Try doing a tiny back and forth rocking movement with your upper body. How does it feel?

- Raise your sternum (breast bone) a little to create a slight arch in your back (below). Try rocking slightly forward and back again. Does the tiny movement feel less fluid and not quite as effortless as before?

- Go back to the middle point, where the sternum is neither up nor down (below), and rock slightly forward and back once more. Keep the movement subtle, so anyone watching would be unaware you were moving. This is neutral pelvis.

- Drop your sternum so that you slump slightly (top right) and try the rocking movement again. How does the movement feel now?

■ This posture should enable you to move effortlessly in perfect balance without the need to push or brace with any other part of the body. The rocking movement will become almost self-maintaining, requiring little if any work on your part.

■ Once in the saddle (or on a saddle horse), find neutral pelvis by placing your legs in front of the saddle flaps and walking forward on your seat bones. You may need someone to hold your horse if he is unsure about movement on his back. Women generally need to walk forward 3mm ($\frac{1}{8}$in) and men generally need to walk back 3mm ($\frac{1}{8}$in). If slight pressure were applied to your sacrum and sternum you would be balanced and more secure in the saddle. Take a piece of the horse's mane in front of the saddle and pull (on a saddle horse, pull on the saddle cloth in front of the pommel). You should feel that your body is completely stable without having to activate any muscle. If you are pulled forward or are bracing through the body you have not found neutral pelvis.

Sarah is now straighter and is no longer sitting behind the vertical

If you are not in neutral pelvis, slight pressure on the sternum will tip you back...

...and slight pressure on the sacrum will tip you forward

Place your legs in front on the saddle flaps and move your seatbones a fraction to find neutral pelvis

When pressure is applied on the sacrum or sternum you will now be stable without having to brace or tighten through the body

You can run through the same checks once on the horse, provided your horse is safe

Floating forward

The energy from the horse's hindquarters and the momentum of the horse's forward movement throws many riders behind the vertical. To compensate for constantly being thrown out of balance, the rider tightens and braces in their upper thighs, hips, lower back and shoulders, which restricts movement through the horse's body. Floating forward is a Connected Riding exercise that helps you to stay straight and light on the horse's back while maintaining equilibrium, allowing him to move freely and effortlessly beneath you.

■ To stay with the horse's movement without your upper body moving excessively backwards and forwards with each stride, find neutral pelvis and then as the horse moves off, float your upper body slightly forward. Staying in neutral pelvis, remember to float slightly forward with every stride. Now the motion of the horse will be automatically balancing your body. It is a minute movement forward and should not be visible to someone on the ground.

Exercises for the horse

In the following pages, the exercises for the horse are arranged under areas of the body. However, if you are looking for a specific exercise, this list should enable you to find it quickly and easily.

Mouth, muzzle and chin

The mouth, muzzle and chin are some of the most expressive parts of the horse and are good indicators of stress levels or concern. A horse that is soft and relaxed in these areas will be calmer and easier to handle and ride.

Mouth work

As far as the horse is concerned, the mouth is often the focus of what he might deem to be constant negative attention: the teeth are floated, paste wormer is shovelled in at frequent intervals and, in the majority of cases, chunks of cold, sometimes uncomfortable, pieces of metal are popped in on a regular basis from the age of four. This often leads to horses being uncomfortable or sensitive in their mouths. The happy news is that with a little knowledge all that can change. The following exercise can bring dramatic improvements to your horse's behaviour and performance and can reduce stress, promote relaxation and increase his concentration span.

Steady the head by holding the headcollar and stroke down the nose and around the mouth and muzzle with the flat of your hand

If your horse is sensitive to contact around the face and muzzle use the back of your hand

> ### This bodywork exercise helps...
> - Prepare a horse to accept the bit
> - Accustom the horse to having his mouth checked for oral imbalance, dental issues or damage
> - Horses that are overly emotional and sensitive
> - Horses that clamp their jaw on the bit
> - Horses that hang on one rein
> - Horses that bite
> - Overcome concerns with paste worming

- Stand slightly to one side of your horse to enable easy access to the mouth area. Steady the head by holding the headcollar and stroke down the nose and around the mouth, muzzle and chin with the flat of your hand. If your horse is sensitive or defensive use the back of your hand. If he dislikes being touched on one side go back to the side that was more comfortable for him, then gradually work your way back around to the other side.

- Once your horse is happy with you working around his mouth, lift the upper lip with your fingers or thumb and, keeping them together, slide your fingers back and forth over the top gum. If his mouth is dry, wet your hand first.

Move the chin gently in circles with the flat of your hand

- If your horse bites or has a strong upper lip, take great care and angle your hand so that the back of the hand is lifting the lip to ensure your fingers remain safely away from his teeth.

■ When working the bottom gums, make small circles with your thumb on the inside of the lip, keeping your fingers outside the horse's chin for support.

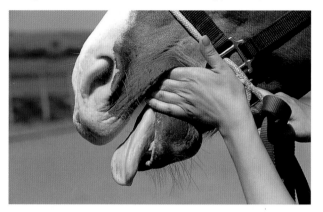

Lift the upper lip with your fingers and slide them back and forth over the upper gum

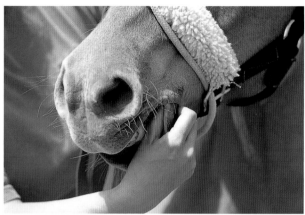

Slide your thumb inside the corner of the mouth and move the cheek gently away from the teeth. Do small circular movements with your thumb

If your horse bites or has a strong upper lip, angle your hand so that the back of your hand is lifting the upper lip

■ Slide your thumb inside the corner of the mouth furthest away from you and make small circles on the inside of the cheek. Move the cheek gently away from the teeth while you do this to avoid being bitten. Check for any lacerations or soreness that may be indicative of a dental problem. Then switch sides.

■ If the horse moves his head around go with the movement rather than restraining him. If he is really concerned try doing TTouches (p.94) somewhere else on the head or the body, or work the ears (p.104). If your horse knows that you will not force him to do anything he finds uncomfortable, trust between you will be established and he will be more willing to let you try again next time.

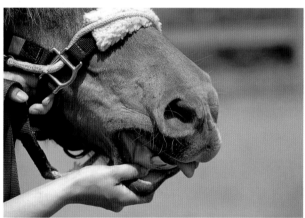

Make small circles along the bottom lips with your thumb

My horse doesn't like mouth work

■ Try nostril work first (p.92)
■ Spend more time moving the lips and muzzle in circular movements with the flat of your hand or the back of your fingers
■ Try stroking the hair of the tail in strands and other tail exercises (pp.130 & 138). The mouth and the tail are linked
■ Put a small light towel around the horse's muzzle and work through the cloth

Spend time moving the lips and muzzle in circular motions

If your horse continues to over-react to having his mouth touched, it may be worth contacting your vet to carry out a thorough examination of the oral cavity, under sedation if necessary, to rule out the possibility of dental problems.

Nostril work

Nostrils vary in size and shape. If the horse is holding tension in his mouth it is likely that the muzzle and the nostrils will also be tight. Working the nostrils can release tight facial muscles, reduce a horse's concern about placing his muzzle through a headcollar noseband and help horses to become more tolerant.

> **This bodywork exercise helps...**
> - Prepare a horse to be tubed, for example in the case of choke or colic
> - Prepare a horse to be handled around the mouth
> - As a starting point for working inside the mouth
> - The horse to gain trust in his handler

- Stand to one side of the horse. Support his head by lightly holding the noseband and cheek piece of the headcollar with your right hand. With your left hand, stroke around the nose and muzzle – gently but with intention – in downward movements with the flat of your hand. If the contact is too light it may irritate the horse and if it is too heavy he may find it uncomfortable. If this is too much for the horse make a soft half open fist with your left hand and use the back of your fingers to do small circular TTouches (p.94) around the nose and muzzle. Be careful to refrain from gripping the headcollar tightly. Also ensure that you are not inadvertently pulling the head down as you concentrate on the work.

- If your horse is happy, continue by sliding the tips of your fingers gently inside the nostril and rubbing its outer edge with your thumb. You can also experiment by sliding your thumb carefully inside the nostril and gently drawing out the edge with your fingers and thumb.

You can also slide your thumb inside the nostril on the opposite side and draw the edge of the nostril gently out

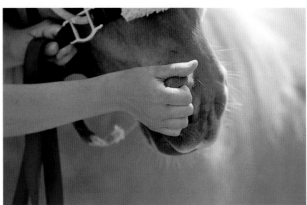

Slide the tips of your fingers inside the nostril

- Work both nostrils from one side by using your thumb inside the opposite nostril or switch sides and repeat the exercise from the other side.

Stroke around the nose and muzzle in downward movements

Meet and melt

When a horse pulls or leans on the bit when we are riding, our natural inclination is to pull back or to try to get him off the bit with a quick correction. A more effective way is to meet the pressure that the horse is applying to the bit and then soften that pressure by slowly melting the contact. As you slowly release, the horse will offer the same response. This encourages him to soften through the jaw and neck and teaches him self-carriage.

> ### My horse doesn't like meet and melt
> - Check you are melting the contact not throwing it away completely
> - Make sure you are meeting the pull with equal pressure before slowly melting
> - Check bit and saddle fit

Stroking the reins

Another way to help the horse release through the jaw, neck and back is to stroke the reins while riding. Either slide the rein through your hand as you turn or try stroking both the reins together with your hands passing one over the top of the other if the horse is bracing and pulling on the bit.

...releasing tension through the jaw, poll, neck and back

> ### My horse doesn't like stroking the reins
> - Check you aren't clamping your legs around his ribs and inadvertently driving him forward
> - Practise neutral pelvis (p.86) and floating forward (p.89)
> - Try the exercises for releasing the neck, back and barrel
> - Check bit and saddle fit

Stroking the reins helps horses that lean on the bit by...

Face, forehead and TMJ (temporomandibular joint)

Horses that are confident and trusting are generally happy to be handled around the head and face. If your horse dislikes contact it is often an indicator of dental problems, tension or the memory of a bad experience. Investing time working around the head and face will relax your horse and deepen the rapport between you.

Move the skin in one and a quarter circles

TTouches

When used on the horse's face, simple circular TTouches help to increase trust, release tight facial muscles and accustom a horse to being handled around the head.

Clouded Leopard TTouch is the foundation for all the circular TTouches. Stand to one side of the horse. Visualize a watch face on the horse's forehead approximately 1cm (½in) in diameter with six o'clock being the lowest point. With one hand lightly holding the lead line or headcollar, take the other hand and place your fingers at six on your imaginary watch face (see diagram). With your fingers in a softly curved position, like a paw, push the skin around the clock in a clockwise circle. Maintain an even pressure all the way round, on past six until you reach eight. At eight, pause for a second and if the horse is relaxed move to another spot and repeat the movement.

- It is important to make only one-and-a-quarter circles each time on any one spot and to ensure that your fingers are pushing the skin in a circle rather than sliding over the hair. When you make a circle rest your thumb lightly against the body to steady the hand. Move your first, second and third fingers as one to ensure that the little finger 'goes along for the ride'. If you tense the joints in your fingers or wrist the movement will become stiff. Allow your fingers to relax and move in the rotation.

> **This bodywork exercise helps...**
> - Calm a nervous horse
> - Horses that are headshy
> - Horses that push with their heads or repeatedly bump their heads
> - Horses that bite
> - Warm cold patches on the nasal bone and face
> - Reduce hot spots
> - Prepare a horse to be haltered and bridled

Pressure levels

The TTouch works on the nervous system and therefore requires relatively little pressure to be effective. Often we are taught from an early age that we must work hard to achieve success. With TTEAM this is simply not the case and it is proven over and over that less is often more. To convey a sense of the amount of pressure that is appropriate when doing the TTouches, TTEAM uses a system of numbers from one to ten.

- Place your thumb lightly on your cheek and gently rest your fingertips on your cheekbone. As lightly as possible move the skin over your cheekbone without rubbing so that you can barely feel the bone underneath your fingers. This is a **one pressure**. Practise by using the same pressure to move the skin on your forearm, noting that there is no indentation on the skin. Moving the skin over the cheekbone with a little more pressure so you can just feel the bone underneath your fingers gives you a **three pressure**. When using a three pressure on the forearm you should notice a slight indentation. Doubling the pressure gives a **six pressure**.

- Clouded Leopard and Raccoon TTouches are most commonly used with a pressure ranging from two to five, depending on the preference of the horse and the area on which you are working. When working around the head and face try using a two or three pressure. Chimp and Llama TTouches are more generally used in a range from two to three.

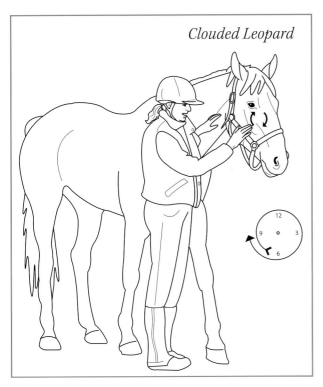

Clouded Leopard

- From the Clouded Leopard position, curve your fingers more so that you are now making the circles with your fingertips. Remember to keep your hand and fingers soft and allow movement through the knuckles.

Llama TTouch suits nervous horses or those that are protective about being touched on certain parts of their body as they may find contact with the back of the hand less threatening.

- Keep your fingers soft and gently stroke the horse's forehead, muzzle and jowl with the back of your fingers. You can also try the circular movements with this TTouch.

Move the skin with the back of your hand if your horse is worried about contact on his face

The Chimp TTouch is useful for nervous or sensitive horses

- Practise doing the circular movements on the back of your hand to soften your hands and give you a sense of how the TTouch differs from other bodywork. It is important to make sure your circles are really round and that they are made in one smooth, flowing movement.

- As you work, remember to breathe. Concentration can cause us to hold our breath, which stiffens our body and affects the TTouch. You can do the Clouded Leopard TTouch around the whole head and face altering your hand position where necessary around the contours of the face to ensure the movement remains fluid and relaxed.

Chimp TTouch This TTouch is particularly useful for nervous horses or for working around the muzzle.

- Make a soft open fist and use the area between the first and second joints on the back of the fingers to move the skin. Keep the hand soft and the fingers together.

Raccoon TTouch is excellent for working around the base of the ear, the eye and around the back of the jowl.

The Raccoon TTouch is excellent for working around the base of the ears

---

My horse doesn't like circular TTouches

- Lighten the pressure. Most people are amazed at how light this work is once they experience it on themselves
- Go in an anti-clockwise direction
- Lightly brush your fingertips over the horse as though you were flicking dust from his face or body. If he settles add the occasional circle
- Speed up or slow down the movement
- Cover your hand with a sheepskin mitt

Angel – Part Two

Continued from p.75. Angel was the first horse we worked with at Akrotiri. Hilary brought her into the arena and when I approached the mare literally flew at me. I wanted to put a lead line over the nose band of Angel's headcollar but it was impossible – all I could do was to clip it quickly onto the side before teeth started snapping and front feet started flying once again. I asked Hilary to take her own lead rope off the bottom ring and clip it onto the other side of the headcollar.

Having Angel between us meant that Hilary could control her while I started initiating contact by touching the mare with a long schooling stick. This minimized the risk of being hurt in an onslaught since at all times we could influence Angel's head position and therefore the rest of her body. Initially, she squealed and struck out with her front legs and protested strongly at my presence, but TTEAM has many practical techniques that enable you to stay safe while working, so there was very little risk of being hurt or of escalating the reactivity in the mare. Angel's behaviour wasn't triggering the responses she had learnt to expect, and she seemed a little thrown by the fact that I was still standing quietly by her. She closed her eyes tightly, so tight that the skin around her lids crinkled. You sometimes see small children do this when they are being told off or feel embarrassed by what a parent is saying to them, and certainly Angel's posture and her breathing revealed she was not closing her eyes because she was relaxing and enjoying the moment. It seemed more as though she was simply pretending – or hoping – I wasn't really there.

After a few minutes stroking Angel down the front legs with the schooling stick, I put my left hand on her neck, keeping my right hand firmly attached to the lead line. Angel's skin was so tight she felt like a drum. Slowly I started moving her skin in the one and a quarter circular Clouded Leopard TTouch (see p.94) and slowly Angel began to change. There were many 'no go' areas on her body that triggered the squealing-striking-snapping I was becoming very familiar with, so I simply worked where I could. By now she could accept contact on the top of her poll, in places on her neck and a little on her shoulder, and she could actually look at me as well. Hilary and I then gave Angel a break. The common beliefs that you 'shouldn't let the horse get away with it' or 'mustn't stop until you get what you want' are neither appropriate nor necessary when working with any horse, particularly when you are using TTEAM. Giving a horse time to process the information and allowing the nervous system to adapt to the gentle work is far more valuable than battling on regardless. It also increases the horse's trust more quickly and prevents stress, fear and fatigue – all of which inhibit the ability to learn – from entering the equation.

When Hilary went back to Angel's pen to get her for a second session, she thought she would have trouble catching her horse as usual, but this time Angel came straight up to her. This is not uncommon. Many times over, horses deemed impossible to catch have been waiting by the gate for a second TTEAM session, much to the amazement of their owners.

In every session Angel became visibly more relaxed. We led her through the labyrinth (see p.132) and over other patterns of poles and interspersed the groundwork with bodywork. Andy joined in, and within seconds he too was able to work virtually all over Angel's body. People had tried to stroke her before but in reality stroking changes very little. There is something magical about those little circular TTouch movements that just melt the tension under your fingertips. It is, however, extremely important to keep your wits about you when working with a horse like Angel and to watch her body language. As Andy turned to me in amazement, her look changed completely and she went for him with her back legs. Seeing it coming, I shouted for him to move and brought her head round so that her hindquarters swung away from him. Andy then went calmly back to working on Angel's body. I think this session was the first time he had ever touched her. The beauty of the bodywork TTouches is that they can bring about lasting changes – often in a very short space of time and as the day progressed Angel began to justify her name.

Hilary takes up the story:

Throughout the day we gave Angel 10–20 minutes bursts of TTEAM work and by the late afternoon she was walking around with Andy and I leading her together. She seemed so much calmer in herself. I was overwhelmed with the difference. We even started introducing the TTEAM body wrap, putting a stretchy bandage around her neck. She accepted this with no fuss which, considering the lead rope issue earlier that morning, seemed quite remarkable.

By the end of the day I was gobsmacked. Never in a million years did I think other people would be able to lead Angel around. I was completely hooked by now and I had learnt absolutely loads. When things were explained it just seemed common sense. I vowed I would continue this work after Sarah left the island. My husband (who is not that horsey) had gained so much confidence around Angel and the other horses that he wanted to become more involved with my 'habit'. The next day Angel let him wash her and even licked his hands.

Three weeks later I have progressed with this amazing technique and my little mare now works with the full body wrap on. Andy works with me as well. He can lead her on his own and does bodywork on her without me having to hold her. I have even encouraged others to take an interest in Angel. She can now be caught easily by a relative stranger and they can work with her on their own with me just sitting watching. I am the proudest owner, and despite Angel's problems, every day I see an improvement in her. It may be small at times but to me it is still significant. This experience has given me such an insight into the way I feel training horses should be. I have never believed in the theory 'beat into submission'. We have no right to hit an animal – I firmly stand by this no matter how frustrating it can get at times.

Update from Sarah Fisher:

Angel never looked back. When Hilary left Cyprus she was able to sell her to another yard. Hilary spent several weeks with Angel's new family teaching children to ride the little mare.

Working with horses like Angel is so rewarding. True aggression is extremely rare. When a horse behaves like Angel it is so easy to label them as dominant, aggressive, mean or mad, but usually they are just plain scared. How many bullies in the human world are truly happy, confident or brave? Being in control of a situation and being controlling are two totally separate things.

Cyprus is always a leveller. It isn't easy there to change saddles, run blood tests, get teeth checked regularly, employ the help of another professional or do any of the things that are routine for me on my yard in England. And still with TTEAM it is totally possible to elicit a complete turn around in a horse's behaviour, in just one day, and these are simple, safe and effective groundwork and bodywork exercises that anyone can learn.

Lowering the head

The position of a horse's head influences how he functions through the rest of his body. When the head is high, the flight/fight reflex is activated. Teaching your horse to lower his head from the ground is an invaluable exercise that will have far reaching benefits. Lowering the head helps horses to connect through their body, reduces sensitivity in the back, improves balance and enables the horse to move beyond his instinctive responses.

> **This groundwork exercise helps...**
> - Increase levels of self-confidence
> - Reduce uneven strain on joints and soft tissue
> - Settle and calm a nervous horse
> - Improve digestion
> - Reduce stress
> - Horses to overcome everyday concerns such as loading, being tied, being groomed and standing quietly for the vet or farrier

There are different ways of teaching a horse to lower his head. Showing him how to release the bracing muscles in the head and neck will quickly enable him to achieve a more desirable posture. However, forcing the head down or training him to stand with a lower head carriage will create bracing through the top and base of the neck.

- If your horse finds it hard to stand still you may want to do this exercise in the stable. Stand on the near side with the soft lead line attached to the headcollar as shown in the following exercise (see p.100) or clip your lead rope to the side of the headcollar. Start slowly and reasonably firmly stroking down the line, alternating between your right and left hand. Cover approximately 20cm (8in) of line with each stroke and start as close to the headcollar as possible. Maintain a contact on the line at all times so that you are constantly drawing it down without pulling. Pay attention to your posture and keep as relaxed as possible through your body. Looking down at the ground and keeping your own body low is more effective than standing braced and upright while looking up into the horse's eye.

To help the horse lower his head try stroking the lead line...

...alternately with your hands

■ You can also try stroking the line with the left hand while the right hand rests gently on the top of the neck near the poll. Do small circular TTouches on the opposite side of the neck with your fingertips or do a gentle squeeze and release on the top of the neck with your fingers and thumb.

If working in hand stroke the lead line...

Another tip is to stroke the lead with one hand while the other hand works on the poll...

...with one hand to help a horse that is braced in the neck or in freeze

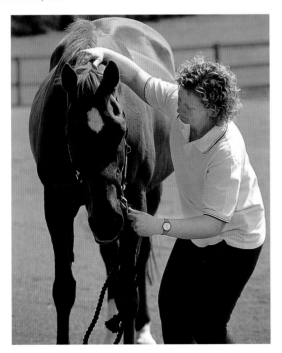

...to encourage the horse to release in the jaw and upper part of the neck

> ### My horse doesn't like lowering his head
> ■ Check you aren't pulling his head down by mistake
> ■ Thread the lead line through the ring on the side of the headcollar, loop it once over the ring and then run the line up the cheekpiece and attach it to the ring by the horse's jowl this ensures that you give more of an ask-and-release signal on the poll and the horse isn't backing away from pressure on the noseband
> ■ Try ear work (p.104) and any of the bodywork and groundwork exercises (pp.112–121) to release the neck

Leading using the wand and TTEAM lead line

A considerable number of horses are taught to stop and move forward purely from a signal on the head. They rarely learn how to organize themselves through the body. The likely result is a horse that works persistently on the forehand and one that relies on the handler or rider for support. This groundwork exercise teaches the horse to slow down, halt, move forward and lengthen and shorten his stride purely from the movement of the wand, which improves focus, balance and adaptability in every horse, regardless of its age.

Leading this way ...
- Increases levels of self-confidence
- Establishes self-carriage
- Improves transitions
- Creates movement and performance that is more thoughtful and more considered
- Reduces uneven stress on joints and soft tissue
- Settles a nervous or reactive horse

Leading with the TTEAM lead line and wand enables a horse to move in self-carriage and to lengthen and release through the neck and back

Attaching the lead line

- Thread the lead line through the side ring on the left side of the horse, from the outside in towards the horse's jaw.

- Run the line up beside the cheekpiece of the headcollar and clip the snap to the ring by the horse's jowl.

- Drop the line down and then take it up and over the noseband of the headcollar. Feed the lead line out through the ring on the opposite side, passing the clip through the ring from the inside to the outside

- If you do not have a TTEAM lead line, use a length of thin climbing rope and tie the end of the rope to the ring by the jowl

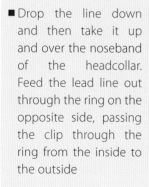

■ Attach the lead line to the side of the headcollar as described opposite. When a signal is given on the lead line, it will produce a light pressure on the nose encouraging the horse to soften at the poll.

As the lead line is looped over the noseband it cannot tighten around the sensitive nasal bone

the chest and front legs. Lift the wand level to the chest again and draw it forward and out, giving a light ask-and-release signal on the lead line at the same time. Give a verbal cue to let the horse know what you want and give him time to organize his body and respond to your request.

■ Keep the contact on the line as light as you can to avoid pulling the horse forward. Repeat the steps if necessary.

■ To stop the horse, move the wand back towards his chest saying 'and....whooa'. Give a little ask-and-release signal back on the lead line if necessary. You can touch the horse's opposite shoulder with the wand to help keep him straight. Keep your feet moving until he halts; if you stop the minute you give the signal, the horse will probably walk past you for a few steps since he needs time to hear and understand the request. By staying up by his nose you can influence the position of his neck and body far more effectively than if you were back by his shoulder. Leading from the shoulder teaches horses to bend their neck to the left and brace through their left shoulder. This quickly becomes an established pattern of movement.

My horse doesn't like being led in this way

■ Make sure you are really clear about what you want and how you are asking him to move
■ Check that you aren't inadvertently keeping pressure on the lead line
■ Make sure he is comfortable in the mouth. Dental changes can make a horse sensitive across the nasal bone.
■ Turn the wand around and use the button end to give the signals (below) – this makes the wand shorter and less of a worry to a horse that may be concerned.

■ Hold the line in your right hand palm up and take the end of the line and your wand in your left hand. Be sure that the line never loops around your fingers or hangs too close to the ground. Stand a little in front of the horse's nose and to the side, holding your wand level with his chest. Move the wand back towards him and, watching for any sign of concern, stroke down

Hold the end of the lead line and the wand in the outside hand picking up the line between your fingers

TTouches around the eye

Working around the eye using simple circular TTouches (p.94) can have a very relaxing effect on the horse. It can release tension in the jaw and is beneficial for horses that are overly emotional or in a constant state of anxiety.

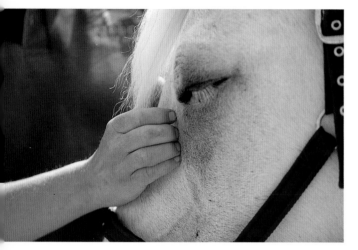

Working around the eye can have a calming and relaxing effect on the horse

My horse doesn't like TTouches around the eye

- Work through the other exercises for the head and face (pp.94–101)
- Use a sheepskin buff
- Try the exercises for releasing tension in the ears and poll (pp.104–111)
- Try cheek delineation (p.106)

Wellington – Part Two

Continued from p.36. As bodywork was difficult for Wellington, freeing up his body and trying to establish some degree of balance through groundwork was the only way forward. Slowly his head began to lower enabling more freedom of movement through the back and hindquarters. Polework, the labyrinth and leading him between two handlers to alter the habitual pattern of falling through the left shoulder made significant changes to his balance in a relatively short space of time. Leading him between two people also had the practical advantage of keeping the handlers safe from striking front feet and we used this exercise to reduce Wellington's suspicion about having people handling him from the offside.

As his physical balance improved, Wellington could tolerate small amounts of bodywork in short sessions, so we added it to the groundwork exercises; shoulder presses and neck releases while on the move helped further improve his head carriage. By listening to the horse and focusing on what he could do rather than on what he could not do, our work began to produce a change in his posture and demeanour. Instead of standing with his head high at all times, Wellington was now resting in his stable with his neck low and relaxed. Transitions became easier and the cow kicking and hollowing under saddle began to diminish. Watching for early warning signs and not punishing the horse for expressing himself built mutual levels of trust in both horse and owner and the squealing and striking when being handled became less frequent.

Within weeks Wellington's neck was softer and he could be groomed in the stable without being haltered, could be mucked out without being removed or tied up and could eat his feed and hay without diving at anyone standing in close proximity. We fed him pro-biotics to help digestion and carried out dental work to remove sharp edges and ramps. This made eating a more comfortable experience for him and helped reduce his sensitivity to smell, enabling us to feed him supplements to support his joints.

He changed saddle size four times in a month and developed muscle over the hindquarters. His neck began to fill and his eye softened and become rounder and shinier. Bloods were taken to check his overall health and to run a rig test, and he barely flinched when the needle entered his vein. The rig test was negative and there were no apparent health concerns that might have attributed to his behaviour. After four months he went to a dressage competition. If at any point he had become upset he would have been withdrawn but not only did he genuinely enjoy his outing, he won one of his classes. The judge's comment at the bottom of the sheet said it all: 'What a calm, obedient test.'

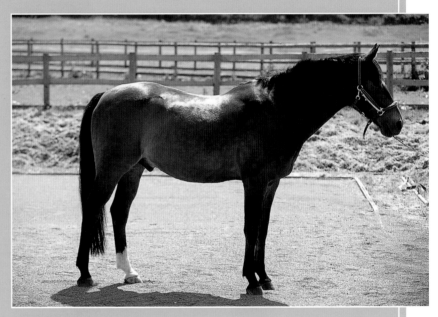

Wellington has made significant improvement and is almost unrecognizable from the horse that arrived at Tilley Farm with a formidable reputation

With Wellington changing so much, the only downside was the saddle fitting, which became a real nightmare. After an exhaustive and demoralizing search, we obtained a Reflex dressage saddle (made by Frank Baines Saddlery, see p.151). This fabulous product has enabled Wellington to remain consistent in the changes he was offering. Even though I thought at one point we had reached a plateau in terms of his physical development, the new saddle allowed his back muscles to develop and strengthen yet again. He is now totally unrecognizable as the horse that first set foot on my yard.

Ears and poll

The majority of horses with quirky, spooky or inconsistent behaviour carry tension around the ears and poll. These areas are susceptible to damage: for example from ear twitching, ear infections, bending or twisting the ear into a bridle, pulling back when tied, hitting the head on a low stable doorway or horsebox and so on. If the horse is relaxed through the base of the ears and around the poll, he will be calmer, easier to handle and more consistent in his performance. Ridden exercises for the neck (see pp.119–121) can also be used to free up the poll.

Lead lines and poll pressure

The majority of the TTEAM and Connected Riding exercises in the following sections release tension through the poll since they are aimed at helping horses to become more flexible and develop the correct posture. The way the lead lines are attached through the side ring of the headcollar also significantly reduces the pressure on the sensitive poll area. Even if you are simply walking your horse out to the field, clipping the lead rope to the side of the headcollar as opposed to the ring at the back of the noseband will give you greater control over the horse and reduce the risk of him rearing or lifting his head against the downward pressure on the poll.

Clipping the lead line on to the side ring of the headcollar reduces pressure on the sensitive poll area and gives you greater control over placement of the horse's head

Ear work

Ear work is a really useful tool that every horse owner should learn. As well as helping to release tension around the base of the ears, the forehead, poll and upper part of the neck, ear work can help horses overcome a variety of issues and may even save lives. It reduces stress, activates the parasympathetic nervous system, lowers the heart rate and respiration, promotes deep, rhythmical breathing, which boosts the immune system, and can stabilize a horse that is fatigued, stressed or going into, or already in, a state of shock. It promotes relaxation and can be done before and after work to calm and settle the horse. Ear work is also an effective way of helping the horse to lower his head and release his poll. Horses that are habitually high headed can really benefit from this work although initially they may be wary.

> **This bodywork exercise helps...**
> - Ear shyness
> - Issues with being bridled and haltered
> - Effects of cold
> - Stiffness
> - Spooky behaviour

- If your horse is happy to have his ears touched, stand in front of him and slightly to one side to avoid being hit in the face if he suddenly startles and raises his head. Work with one ear at a time and support the horse's head with a light contact on the noseband. It is important to rest the fingers on the noseband rather than gripping the noseband. This way you can easily let go if the horse needs to move. If you are working with the horse's left ear you will stroke the ear with your right hand and rest the fingers of your left hand on the headcollar and vice versa.

■ Holding the ear gently but firmly, stroke the ear from the base right out to the tip. Move the position of your hand each time to ensure that the whole ear is covered with the strokes. Work gently but with intent. If you are too tentative you may make your horse nervous, particularly if he is ear shy.

Stand in front of the horse and stroke the ear from the base...

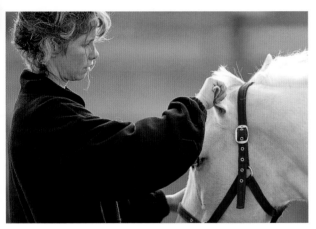

...to the tip

Shock point

The shock point is found on the tip of the ear. Working it by making circular movements on the tip of the ear with the finger and thumb is beneficial for horses that have had a traumatic experience, have cold tips to their ears and/or are habitually nervous.

■ The speed with which you work will vary on the horse's response and the situation. To calm a nervous horse and to promote relaxation, work quite slowly. If your horse is unsure, start by working more quickly initially and then gradually slow the movements as he settles. With a horse that is fatigued, or to bring a horse round from sedation, work a little more quickly.

My horse doesn't like ear work

■ Start by standing to one side as this is often less threatening to a nervous horse. Work the ear nearest to you then switch sides.

■ If your horse is still concerned try stroking the ear gently but with intention back against the top of his neck with the back of your hand (right). Some horses find it more acceptable having their ear touch their own body initially.

■ Try covering your hand with a glove or sheepskin buff.

■ Try holding the ear near its base and very gently take it slightly out to the side, pause for a moment and then slowly guide it back.

■ Try the other exercises in this section and also exercises for the neck (pp.112–121) and mouth (pp.90–93).

Cover your hand with a sheepskin buff

Try holding the base of the ear and gently draw the ear slightly out to the side

Cheek delineation

This simple and effective Connected Riding poll-releasing exercise improves mobility through the horse's entire body and enables lateral movement through the neck to become more even. Many horses have tension through the poll, which affects the TMJ, the neck, the back and the hindquarters.

> **This bodywork exercise helps...**
> - The horse to lengthen and release his entire neck
> - Improve engagement
> - Encourage more movement through the shoulders
> - Release the TMJ, which helps the horse to be quieter in the mouth, both in hand and under saddle

- Stand on the left side of the horse, facing the jowl. Place your left hand on the horse's nose over the noseband of the headcollar; alternatively, hold the lead line with your hand, up by side ring of the headcollar. The second option is more appropriate with horses that have a tendency to mouth or bite as it enables you to keep the horse's head away from you. Using your right hand, place your index, middle and ring fingers in the groove just below the horse's ear at the top of the cheekbone. Slowly run your fingers down the groove following the line of the cheekbone. Repeat a few times feeling for areas that are tight or blocked. Switch sides.

> **My horse doesn't like cheek delineation**
> If your horse finds it hard to open through the throatlatch area, he may find this exercise uncomfortable at first. Try:
> - Walking your fingertips down the groove
> - Ear work (p.104)
> - Clouded Leopard TTouches (p.94) and Racoon TTouches (p.95) around the whole area
> - The chin rest exercise (p.110)
> - Exercises to release the neck (pp.112–121)

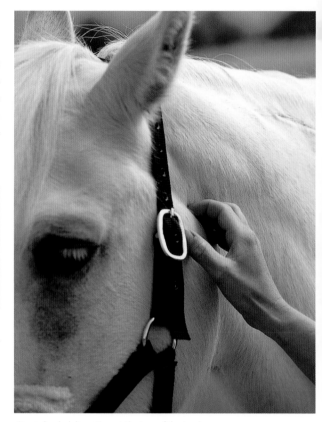

Start cheek delineation at the top of the jowl...

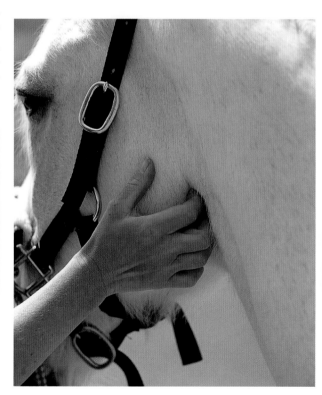

...and run your fingers slowly down the groove following the line of the cheekbone

Cheek press

This is another Connected Riding exercise that helps you to assess whether the horse has the ability to release and move his head, through releasing his poll and upper part of the neck.

> **This bodywork exercise helps...**
> - Create more brain/body awareness
> - Improve stride length and fluidity of movement
> - Encourage more even rein contact
> - The horse to develop better balance and co-ordination
> - The horse to become more active through the pelvis and hind limbs

- Stand on the left side of the horse's head, facing the side of his jowl. Place your left hand on the bridge of his nose, over the noseband. Make a loose fist with your right hand and place it in the centre of the horse's cheek. Keep your wrist straight to maintain an even connection with the horse. Check your posture and make sure that your hips and knees are soft.

Place one hand on the nasal bone. Make a loose fist in the centre of the horse's cheek with the other

- Start with a pause to allow the horse to become accustomed to having your hands on his head. If the horse is happy for you to be handling him in this way, continue with the exercise. The left hand is going to invite his head slightly towards you and the right hand will suggest that the cheek move slightly away from you. The movements are small. Apply a small amount of pressure through the right hand while asking the nose to move slightly towards you with the left hand.

Maintaining this position, pause for a moment to see if the horse begins to soften and release through the poll. Release the pressure on the cheek and soften the contact on the nose very, very slowly. Repeat the exercise a few times, gradually increasing the pressure each time, before switching sides.

Watch for signs of softening and release

- Make sure you aren't forcing the movement in any way or applying downward pressure on the nose. The idea is to suggest the movement rather than making the movement happen. By rotating your pelvis slowly to the left then pausing before rotating slowly back to the right, you will encourage more release through the neck and prevent tension building up in your shoulders and arms.

- As the horse releases you should feel him soften under your hand. He may close his eyes, start breathing deeply, sigh, or there may be a nasal discharge. Sometimes horses shake their head after this exercise.

> **My horse doesn't like cheek press**
> If your horse is unsettled with this exercise try:
> - TTouches around the head and face (pp.94–95 & 102)
> - Forelock circles and slides (p.108)
> - Ear work (p.104)
> - Releasing the neck by working from the base of the neck up with the caterpillar (p.113)
> - Doing other exercises for releasing tension in the neck, such as neck rocks (p.112) and mane slides (p.114)
> - Having his teeth checked

Forelock circles and slides

Stroking the horse's forelock strand-by-strand and circling the forelock can start releasing tension from the ears and poll. It also helps to relax the forehead and TMJ and prepares the horse for forelock pulls (p.115), which can encourage the horse to lengthen and soften his neck and back. This is a really simple exercise that the majority of horses enjoy and that many horse owners and handlers do instinctively. It can also been done when the horse is bridled.

> **This bodywork exercise helps...**
> - Reduce concerns over the bridle and headcollar
> - Horses to gain trust
> - Teach a horse to lower his head
> - Improve a horse's balance

Rest your fingers lightly on the noseband; avoid gripping

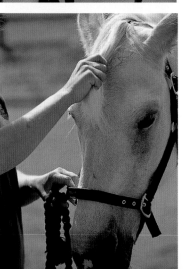

Stroke the hair lightly from the base to the tip

■ Stand in front of your horse and slightly to one side. Rest one hand lightly on the noseband of the headcollar or bridle. Remember to keep your fingers open and refrain from tightening your grip around the noseband, so your hand can slide easily off the headcollar if your horse flings up his head. Using the other hand, gently take a strand of the forelock and stroke the hair lightly from the base right out to the end. The aim is to relax the horse and to release tension from between the ears, the forehead and around the forelock and poll, so ensure that you work slowly and calmly. Work the entire forelock in this manner. Watch to see if there is movement through the skin around the forelock – if the horse carries a lot of tension in this area there may be minimal movement through this area at first but it should increase as the horse begins to relax.

■ Once your horse is happy with forelock slides, hold the forelock close to the roots and gently and slowly circle it both clockwise and anticlockwise. Note whether the horse prefers a particular direction and watch his eye and ear set for any signs of concern.

> **My horse doesn't like forelock slides and circles**
> - Try breaking the exercise down into simpler steps and note at which point your horse finds it uncomfortable.
> - Try the exercise by standing to one side of the horse
> - Place the back of your hand on the horse's forehead over the forelock and circle your hand gently in one and a quarter circles (right)
>
> - Try clockwise circles initially but if your horse doesn't settle try anti-clockwise circles
> - If your horse is still concerned, wear a sheepskin grooming mitt on your hand and try again
> - Try the exercises for the mouth (pp.90–93) and neck (p.112–121) and work slowly towards the poll
> - Try ear work (p.104)

Tracing the arc

This simple exercise can highlight and help any imbalance between the left and right rein. It reduces tension in the poll, TMJ and neck, and will also help the horse to develop straightness and even rein contact.

> **This bodywork exercise helps...**
> - Horses that have issues about being handled around the poll
> - Horses that evade the bit when on a particular rein
> - The horse to develop more body awareness
> - Encourage better hind limb engagement
> - Establish flexion through the neck without falling through the shoulder

- The noseband needs to be relatively snug for this exercise. Stand in front of your horse with your thumb and index fingers hooked near the middle of the noseband or supporting the noseband lightly with both hands. The horse's neck should be as straight as possible. Imagine an arc that begins and ends in line with the shoulders of the horse. You are standing at the top or in the middle of the arc.

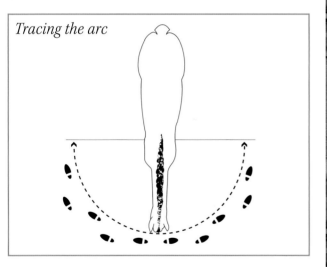

Tracing the arc

- Take one small step to the left. Pause to allow the horse to release his head and poll. Slowly take one or two more small steps to the left taking the horse's head gently with you and pausing to allow for the release each time. Your feet will be following the line of the imaginary arc. Then take small steps to the right still pausing and allowing

As you do this exercise, note whether the horse finds it easier to move in one direction. This mare is only turning from the poll, not through the neck and she is disconnecting when moving to the left

for the release until you are back where you started. Repeat the exercise stepping to the right this time.

■ Remember to soften through your knees, hips and back and keep your arms light. If you lean on the headcollar you will encourage your horse to brace more through the neck to compensate for your lack of balance.

■ You are aiming for fluidity of movement although at the beginning you may feel that your horse gets 'stuck' or that the movement is jerky. Note whether your horse finds it easier to move in one direction to the other. This will correspond to the way he moves under saddle.

■ You may only be able to achieve a few steps in both directions at first but as your horse begins to release through the poll and through the neck you should be able to increase the range of movement by moving further along the curve of the imaginary arc.

My horse doesn't like tracing the arc
- Check your own posture to ensure that you aren't bracing and creating tension in your hand
- Make the movements really small by taking tiny steps to the left and to the right
- Increase the length of the pause to allow the horse to process the information and release his neck
- Use the neck exercises (pp.112–121) to release the neck from the base to the poll
- Try mouth work (p.90) to help the horse increase his focus
- Use the walking the 'S' exercise (p.118) to release the poll and neck while on the move
- Try forelock circles and slides (p.108)

Chin rest

This exercise helps horses open through the throatlatch and poll. You can do it while stationary or when walking your horse in hand.

This groundwork exercise helps...
- Horses that hold onto or lean onto the bit
- Horses that tilt their head
- Encourage forward movement into a contact
- Release the shoulders

■ Hold the lead line in the outside hand and use the hand nearest the horse to support the chin groove. The aim is to encourage him to release into your hand. Keep your posture relaxed and soften your knees and hips. Think about moving from your feet, which will allow the horse to soften and go with the movement. If you try and steer him purely through your hand you will encourage him to brace more through the poll and neck.

Hold the lead line in the outside hand and use your inside hand to support the chin groove

Allow the horse to release and lower his head into your hand. The position of this horse's ears show that lowering his head is hard for him

---

My horse doesn't like the chin rest
- Check your outside hand is not inadvertently lifting the lead line up in the air
- Soften your contact on the chin groove and introduce the exercise while the horse is standing still
- Work through all the exercises for releasing tension in the face and neck (pp.94–121)

Zigzag poles

This groundwork exercise can be done with a minimum of six poles if necessary. A good awareness exercise, it encourages the horse to soften and yield at the poll and therefore through the rest of the body. It is excellent for horses that are really stiff as it is not very demanding. The angles can be altered to suit each horse, and poles can be added to increase the length of the exercise.

- Lay out the poles as shown. Attach the lead line as described on p.100 or attach your rope to the side of the headcollar. Hold the lead line in your right hand near the headcollar, with the rest of the rope in your left hand. If your horse is habituated to being handled from the near side start by leading him from here. Position yourself up by his nose so that you can guide him around the turns.

- Start walking slowly. Keep your hips and knees soft and allow the movement to come from your feet up into the lead line. If you brace through the shoulders and try to push or pull the horse around the turns he will fall out of balance.

- As you zigzag the horse through the turns note whether it is easier for him to turn in a particular direction, whether he tilts his head, gets stuck, speeds up as he turns or falls out through the shoulder. Be aware of how heavy he feels in your hand.

Use the wand to give a forward signal and stay up by the horse's nose to allow him to walk through the exercise in self-carriage

- When he has happily walked through the poles once, repeat the exercise but this time halt him just before each turn. Lead him into the zigzag arrangement from both directions and switch the side you lead from. See if this makes a difference to the horse. Experiment with different speeds and see whether he can creep through the poles one small step at a time or whether he can shorten or lengthen his stride as you shorten and lengthen yours.

- If your horse rushes or panics, he is concerned or unclear about what is being asked of him. Let him walk out over the poles and quietly ask him to try again. The aim is to move him slowly through the exercise and to increase the angle as you progress so that each turn encourages more flexibility. You are aiming to have a horse that becomes light in the hand, can turn relatively evenly in both directions and can soften and yield through the poll and the neck on each bend.

My horse doesn't like zigzag poles

- Start by leading your horse past a single pole on the ground. Then add a second pole to the end of the first at a slight angle. Gradually build up the exercise this way until he is happily walking and stopping next to a line of three or four poles. Add the parallel line of poles one at a time, keeping the space between the two sets of lines really wide. When the horse is happily working in a wide zigzag, start reducing the space.

Ask the horse to halt between the poles

Neck

A tight or incorrectly developed neck is one of the primary causes of stress, unwanted behaviour and poor function in the horse. If the neck is tight it will be impossible for him to work in balance, develop a supple back and release and lengthen his top line. Spending even a few minutes a day working on your horse's neck will help him to become easier to handle and train, more focused, happier and more connected to every other part of his body. As a horse begins to free up in the upper part of the neck, you may notice a discharge from one or both of his nostrils.

Dave is a young horse and still lacks a top line. When he draws back his neck he cannot move forward freely and spooks at objects on the ground

To achieve and maintain a free and well-developed neck...

- Warm up thoroughly
- Allow plenty of stretching at intervals during ridden work
- Refrain from working in a collected frame for long periods of time
- Avoid tying down the horse's head to create an illusion of a correct outline
- Avoid tight nosebands
- Increase the difficulty of the exercises and ridden work slowly
- Teach the horse to develop true self-carriage
- Ensure the teeth and feet are well cared for and any imbalances are corrected at regular intervals
- Refrain from plaiting too tightly and only plait on the day of the competition
- Ensure the saddle fits correctly and is not placing pressure on the wither area or back, which will trigger the neck to rise
- Feed hay from the floor
- Cool down thoroughly

Neck rock

This is a really simple TTEAM exercise that most horses will accept, at least in places, straight away. It relaxes tight ligaments and muscles, helps to release a tight bottom line, connects the top line to the bottom line and is one step on the path to true balance and straightness.

This bodywork exercise helps...
- The horse become accustomed to having his neck handled
- Start the steps to teaching a horse to lower his head and neck
- The horse to release the withers, shoulders, back, poll and jaw

- You can do this exercise by standing on either side of the horse; here it is described as though you were working by the horse's offside. Start the exercise anywhere on the horse's neck. If you can work from the bottom all the way up to the poll or start at the poll and work down to the base of the neck, so much the better. Some horses are so tight in the neck that they can only tolerate contact in certain places but after a few neck rocks in an acceptable area the neck usually releases enough to allow you to work the whole neck.

Place your hands on the top and bottom of the neck and jiggle it gently to release tension

- Stand in balance with your feet shoulder-width apart and your hips and knees soft. Place the palm of your left hand on top of the crest and the palm of your right hand underneath the neck. Keep your hands in line with each other. Let your fingers firmly but gently cup the top and bottom of the neck. Refrain from gripping tightly.

- Bring the crest slightly towards you with your left hand as you move the bottom of the neck slightly away from you with the right hand, then guide the crest away from you with the left hand as your right hand brings the bottom of the neck towards you. Do this quite quickly so that you are in fact jiggling or rocking the neck.

My horse doesn't like neck rock

Break the exercise into steps:
- Rock him gently from the withers with one hand (p.124)
- Place one hand on the crest and keep the other hand off the horse
- Gently rock the crest but keep the contact light and the movement small
- Place the second hand on the underside of the neck and close the fingers of both your left and right hand slowly and gently around the horse's neck, hold for a moment and then release
- Half rock the neck – that is only move the neck lightly once in one direction before moving to another area
- Try the other exercises for releasing tension in the neck

The caterpillar

The caterpillar is a Connected Riding exercise that can be done while the horse is standing or on the move. It reduces soft tissue tension around the cervical vertebrae, helps the horse to lengthen and release his neck, and helps to establish true self-carriage.

This bodywork exercise helps...
- Teach a horse to soften and accept a contact
- Establish lateral movement in the body
- Reduce a horse's tendency to brace the neck and fall through the shoulder
- The horse to release and yield from the poll right through to the hindquarters

---

- If working on the left side of the horse, support his head by hooking your fingers lightly onto the noseband or by holding the lead line up by the headcollar with your left hand. Place your right hand on the base of the horse's neck above the point of the shoulder. Your thumb should be on or near the jugular groove, and your fingers should be on the top ridge of the cervical vertebrae so that you cup the vertebrae with your hand.

- Start by sliding your hand up the line of the vertebrae to the horse's ear with the base (heel) of the hand applying the pressure. Repeat, but this time move your hand like a caterpillar, inching your way up the neck, vertebra by vertebra. Finally, add the action of opening and closing your thumb and fingers as you travel up the neck.

Support the lead line in the outside hand and use your other hand to work up the line of the vertebrae from the base of the neck to the poll

Experiment with the pressure as it will vary from horse to horse. Repeat this exercise four or five times, giving your horse time to process the information, before switching sides.

Working on Dave's neck under saddle helps him to release and relax

> **My horse doesn't like the caterpillar**
> - Try doing the exercise with the horse walking in hand
> - Start by working only where contact on the neck is acceptable for the horse
> - Alter the pressure
> - Ensure that you aren't pulling on the horse's head by mistake
> - Try the other exercises to release tension around the ears and poll (pp.104–111)

Mane slides

This is another quick and simple TTEAM exercise to help your horse begin to relax and loosen a tight crest and nuchal ligament.

- Stand on any side of the horse, holding the lead line or headcollar in one hand. Take a small piece of mane between the fingers and thumb of your other hand and, holding it near its base, gently circle it in both directions. Slowly slide your fingers up the strands of hair, taking the mane in a straight line from the crest if the mane is short. If it is long, slide your fingers up the hair in a straight line for a little way and then continue with the slide following the strand as it falls down the neck.

> **This bodywork exercise helps...**
> - A horse overcome issues with plaiting, having his mane shortened or detangled
> - Teach a horse to lower and lengthen his neck
> - Develop a correct top line
> - Promote relaxation in horses that find it hard to stand still

When you do the circles and slides watch the skin over the neck, withers and shoulders. You may be amazed at how large an area is influenced by this simple work.

Take the mane and circle the hair in both directions

(Above) If the mane is long stroke the hair down following the natural fall of the hair

(Left) Slide your fingers up the hair to the end

> **My horse doesn't like mane slides**
> - Stroke the tail hair first to release the back and promote a sense of calm
> - Use the other neck-release exercises
> - Try mouth work (p.90) to release the TMJ and poll
> - Do ear work (p.104)
> - Stroke the tips of the mane hair lightly without creating any pull on the skin

Forelock pulls

Adapted from TTEAM tail work, this exercise has proved an excellent addition to the exercises aimed at releasing and lengthening a horse's neck. Forelock pulls also create movement through the entire top line. They can be done as part of the bodywork routine, or prior to or during ridden work. This exercise is especially good for horses that find it hard to work on a free rein.

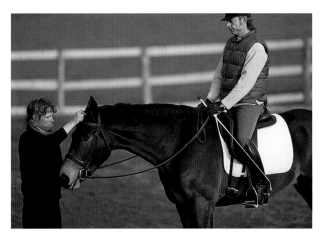

Forelock pulls on a horse under saddle helps to release the neck and lift the back

guiding the movement back to where it started. The release needs to be the longest part of this exercise. Look at the withers, chest muscles, shoulders and back while you are working. You should see movement through the entire body, although some horses are so blocked to begin with that the movement is minimal or restricted to certain parts of their body.

Hold the forelock with one hand and gently rock your weight onto your back foot. Pause and slowly release by rocking your weight forwards

---

This bodywork exercise helps...

- To free the shoulders, ribs and withers
- Prepare a horse to be bridled
- Horses that dislike being caught
- Horses that are tight or unevenly developed through the temporal muscles
- Teach a horse to lower his neck
- Horses that are ear shy

- Stand in front of your horse and slightly to one side. Place one foot in front of the other. Rest one hand lightly on the noseband of the headcollar or bridle. Remember to keep your fingers open and refrain from tightening your grip around the noseband.

- Gently take the forelock and stroke the hair lightly from the base right out to the end. If your horse is happy, return to the base and this time keep hold of the forelock. Gently rock your weight onto your back foot and draw your horse's neck towards you. Hold for a moment and then slowly transfer your weight onto your front foot,

---

My horse doesn't like forelock pulls

- Do forelock circles and slides (p.108) and other exercises to release the neck
- Start with tail work (pp.130 & 138)
- Work him in hand through the labyrinth (p.132) or leading him in an 'S' (p.118)
- Try mouth work (p.90) and circular TTouches (p.94) around the head, face, upper neck and poll
- Stand to one side of the horse and making the movements really small — almost as though you are imagining the movement as opposed to actually drawing the forelock forward

...o lead between two people is very
ben... only habituates a horse to be led from
both sides ... can encourage straightness and balance.
It teaches a horse to walk in his own space and not follow
or lean on his handler for support and enables people to
work with reactive horses safely and quietly. Although
there are two handlers only one is primarily going to be
influencing the horse. The second person acts as a neutral
support and is there when needed. It's a little like flying
a plane. One person is the pilot, the other the co-pilot. If
both people are fighting to control the plane and giving
conflicting signals, it is likely to end in a crumpled mess.

- Both handlers hold wands in their outside hand along
with the end of the lead line. The primary handler
gives the signals with the wand and can back up
the signal with a light ask-and-release signal on the
line if necessary. The aim is to teach the horse to
alter his balance with a signal from the wand rather
than a pull on his head. This helps the horse to work
in self-carriage and is an excellent exercise for teaching
self-control.

> **This groundwork exercise helps...**
> - Horses that crowd the handler or spin
> - Horses that are concerned about walking between narrow spaces
> - Horses that have concerns about being handled by more than one person
> - Teach a horse how to stand
> - Improve handling skills and communication

- With a very forward-going horse, to minimize the chance
of you pulling back on the lead line, ensure the hand
holding the line nearest the headcollar is forward. This
will also remind you to stay as far forward as you can.

- Work in walk until you are used to the exercise then
start using poles, such as the labyrinth (p.132). Position
yourselves slightly in front of the horse's nose so that
you can see each other. To ask for walk, the primary
handler strokes the horse on the chest and down the
front legs with the wand and then draws the wand
forward and out, level with the horse's chest. If the horse
doesn't move forward, repeat this step and give a little
ask-and-release forward on the lead line at the same
time. If the horse is stuck, one of the handlers can bring

Attaching two lead lines
- Attach the first lead rope as described on p.100.

- Take a second
lead line and
thread it through
the ring on the
other side of the
headcollar.

- Then back
through the ring
from the inside.
This prevents the
ring from tipping
into the horse's
face.

- Bring it around
to the outside
and between
the other lead
line and the
cheekpiece

- Twist the line
and attach it
back on itself.
This stops a loop
being created,
which could
cause a problem
if the horse gets
loose.

the horse's head a little towards them to release his neck and shoulder. Be clear about who is going to influence the horse's head as two people pulling in opposite directions will be confusing.

My horse doesn't like the homing pigeon
- Try the alternative system (below)
- Work in hand with one person doing shoulder presses (p.126) and the caterpillar (p.113)
- Do the other exercises to release the neck and those that work on the withers and shoulders (pp.122–135)

The aim is to teach the horse to walk quietly between two handlers on loose lines

- An alternative system for the second handler is to use a long length of thin climbing rope slipped through the headcollar ring on the offside. You do not use a wand, as the ends of the line are held separately in each hand. The length of the rope enables you to stay further away from the horse and by gently drawing each end of the line back and forth you can teach him to soften to the sensation. As the line is not attached, it can be quickly slipped out of the ring if the horse panics.

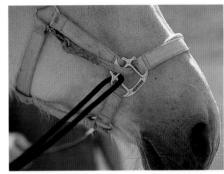

Using a length of thin climbing rope threaded through the ring is excellent for teaching youngsters to lead and helps accustom nervous or crooked horses to being led between two people

If the horse braces or goes into freeze, one of the handlers can give a little ask-and-release signal on their line to unlock the poll enabling him to move forward quietly

The second handler can stay further away

- The second handler keeps a neutral support on their line and has their wand forward and out. The wands should be level with each other with the tips pointing towards each other without touching to form an open-ended triangle. To slow a fast-moving horse, one handler can bring the wand back part way towards the horse's chest and then open the wand again so that they can repeat the movement if required.

- The primary handler needs to give clear instruction to both the horse and the second handler as to where they are going and when they are going to prepare to halt and move on.

By sliding the line a little as you walk you can suggest straightness rather than forcing it

Free up your horse

Walking the 'S'

This Connected Riding exercise can be done while walking your horse out to and in from the field, on the way to the mounting block or in the school prior to mounting as part of a warm-up routine. Walking the 'S' softens and releases the horse's neck, encourages the ribs to open and the back to lift. It encourages a more even rein contact and helps the horse to release the jaw and poll, which enables more elevation and connectivity through the body.

> ### This groundwork exercise helps...
> - Horses that are stiff and one-sided
> - Horses that crowd or lean on the handler
> - Encourage more even weight distribution through the limbs

- Stand at your horse's head on the left side. With your right hand, either hold the lead line up next to the headcollar or hook your fingers through the noseband of the headcollar or bridle. Check your posture; ensuring your knees, hips and back are soft.

- The loops of the S should be shallow to begin with. Start the S by rotating your pelvis to the right and walking a few steps with the horse, this flexes him to the right as he moves. Walk four or five strides without making too much of a curve then, continuing walking, slowly rotate your body to the left taking four or five strides. Repeat this pattern and if the horse is able to release with ease gradually increase the depth of the loop.

...then walk to the right. Increase the depth of the loop as you progress through the exercise

- As the depth of the loop increases you may need to step back a stride as you rotate back to the left. The aim is to keep a light connection through your hand and to encourage the horse to soften and yield in a fluid movement.

> ### My horse doesn't like walking the S
> - Do the zigzag poles (p.111) and the labyrinth (p.132)
> - Try freeing up his poll and neck with the appropriate exercises (pp.104–121)
> - Practise on another horse to see if you need to refine your technique

Begin the exercise by rotating your body to the right and sending the horse away from you as you walk...

The neck ring

Linda Tellington Jones has used riding with [...] her work for many decades. In the mid-19[...] the United States of America giving de[...] brideless riding and jumping. The nec[...] p.82) is an excellent way of improving the [...] the horse and rider and can be used to [...] to soften and yield through every part [...] the appropriate steps to ensure safety, [...] removed completely.

The neck ring helps horses to releas[...] carriage and self-confidence. It is als[...] easy to learn that even a child can ma[...] one session.

> **This ridden exercise helps...**
> - Horses that spook
> - Horses that tilt their head or fall through the shoulde[...]
> - Horses that lean or hold on to the bit
> - High-headed horses

- Do this exercise in an enclosed area. Ensure that the horse will not spook if he sees the neck ring out of the corner of his eye by introducing it from the ground. Lead him from one side and then the other and get him used to the feel of the neck ring on his neck by giving a little sideways ask-and-release to turn, while holding the reins with the outside hand.

- If your horse is unconcerned, put the reins back over the head and mount. You can knot the reins and hold them in one hand while the other hand holds the neck ring. Give an ask-and-release signal on the side of the neck to turn. You may need to experiment with signalling on different parts of the neck to see where is most effective. Avoid twisting the neck ring or pulling the horse round with it. If your horse drops his neck too low give a little upwards ask-and-release signal on the underside of the neck near the throatlatch area.

- Signal for halt with the reins and the neck ring combined with your voice command 'whooaa'. In addition, teach your horse that the signal to stop includes a movement that closes your upper thighs on him as well as the rein aid, voice and the signal from the ring. Be very aware of keeping the lower leg below the mid-calf away

Ask for a bend by giving an ask-and-release signal on the opposite side of the neck

Free up your horse

Fish – Part Two
Continued from p.51. Teaching Fish a new way [...]
functioning through groundwork, bodywor[...]
ridden exercises enabled him to change [...]
pattern. With his head carriage unna[...]
was often in the flight/fight reflex [...]
under saddle or in his stable. T[...]
lower his head helped to re[...]
neck. In turn this enable[...]
his hindquarters to [...]
work was carried [...]
that were inhi[...]
he was fitt[...]
change[...]
in-h[...]

After going through specific steps to ensure that it was safe...

... of ... and ... his habitual ... turally high he ..., whether in hand, ... eaching Fish how to ... ease and lengthen his ... his back to lift and allowed ... ork more effectively. Dental ... ut to remove the ramps and hooks ... biting movement of his lower jaw and ... d for a wider saddle that allowed all the ... to take place. The walking the S was an easy ... nd exercise for Maggs to do with Fish if he felt ... reatened when working with other horses in the arena, and it helped him to settle and focus.

As his posture improved a dramatic change in his behaviour occurred: the flight/fight behaviour virtually disappeared. Fish became easier and more consistent to ride, and a happier and more contented horse all round.

from your horse since this will encourage him to keep moving forward. Once he has learnt to stop easily, you can leave the reins alone and turn and slow down solely from the neck ring. By going through appropriate steps to work safely without the bridle, the horse can be ridden with just the neck ring.

...Fish is now being ridden without his bridle

My horse doesn't like the neck ring

- Try the exercises to release the neck, shoulders and back
- Check that you aren't squeezing with your lower leg
- Check that you aren't just pulling on the neck ring
- Introduce the balance rein (p.128) from the ground and progress to the neck ring

Crest releases

This TTEAM exercise generally only needs to be done for a few moments under saddle before it begins to initiate changes in the horse's posture. Crest releases encourage the horse to lower and lengthen his neck, which in turn helps him to lift his back and engage his hindquarters.

This ridden exercise helps...

- Horses that are nervous and spooky
- Horses that find it hard to release into a soft contact
- Improve the stride length

- Take the reins in one hand and place the other hand on top of your horse's neck, palm down with your fingers and thumb either side of the crest. Push your hand up the crest from the base of the neck towards the head. Only go as far as you can comfortably and safely. If your horse has a habit of flinging his head high, start by working on the lower part of the neck to avoid being smacked in the face.

My horse doesn't like crest releases

- Check your lower leg isn't moving backwards against his sides as you push your hand up the crest
- Check the bit, teeth and saddle fit
- Try using the balance rein (p.128) or neck ring (p.119) instead
- Start with groundwork and do the caterpillar (p.113) and shoulder delineation (p.123) before mounting
- If possible start by doing the exercise when the horse is standing still

---

Dan uses the crest releases to help Dave lengthen his top line

Shoulders and chest

The shoulders and chest reflect what is happening through the neck and back, and influence stride length both in front and behind. Work that helps to keep them moving freely will enable the horse to lift through the back and engage his hindquarters.

Front leg circles

Moving a horse's front legs in small clockwise and anti-clockwise circles can loosen stiff shoulders and release the neck and upper part of the back. It can increase circulation to the lower limb and hoof and is a quick and easy way of helping horses that are stabled for long hours in winter and elderly horses that stiffen up during colder weather. Leg circles can be done when the hooves are picked out. You may find that the horse can circle some legs more easily than others or is significantly stiffer through one limb.

> **This bodywork exercise helps...**
> - Develop a more even gait
> - Encourage hind limb engagement
> - The horse to lower his neck and release his top line
> - Improve balance
> - Loading and travelling issues

- Standing on the near side, support the front fetlock joint with your left hand and the hoof with your right hand. Keep your thumb on top of the hoof wall or shoe to minimize the risk of being caught in the face if the horse lifts his leg. Supporting the fetlock prevents tension being placed on this joint. Rest your right elbow on your right knee or thigh to prevent tension in your back. Make sure your feet are in a position that enables you to stand in balance and away from the hoof in case the leg is snatched back and put down. Circle your body slowly to get the movement through the leg. Keep the range of movement small – taking the leg as far as it will go will cause bracing. Repeat on the offside.

Support the fetlock joint with the inside hand and cradle the hoof with the right hand

Rest your outside elbow on your outside knee and circle the leg in both directions

Shoulder delineation

This exercise is used in TTEAM and Connected Riding. It helps horses to alter habitual patterns of bracing through the shoulder and base of the neck and is useful for improving the horse's ability to transfer his centre of gravity in transitions. Shoulder delineation is also helpful for horses that fall through the shoulder or for those that have a short or irregular stride.

This bodywork exercise helps...

- Improve hind limb engagement
- Release the jaw
- Horses that work above or behind the vertical
- Prepare a horse to work with the balance rein (p.128) or neck ring (p.119)
- Horses that struggle with travelling or the farrier

- Start on the near side of the horse. Face forward and hold the lead line in your left hand. If your horse is likely to mouth or bite, hold the line up by the headcollar. Keep your knees soft and your body slightly rotated and folded at the hip. Place your fingers at the top of the shoulder just below the withers in the front ridge of the shoulder blade. With your fingers together and pointing downwards, follow the line of the groove in front of the shoulder blade. Curve your fingers and continue down the groove. You will probably notice the shoulder is less easily delineated at the top and the bottom of the groove. This will be linked in part to how your horse has been bracing through the base of his neck, chest and shoulders. If there are tight areas, bring the horse's head slightly towards you to encourage more of a release. Repeat a couple of times and then switch the lead line to the other side and work on the opposite shoulder.

My horse doesn't like shoulder delineation

- Walk your fingertips lightly down the groove
- Do small circular TTouches (p.94) around the whole shoulder area
- Rock the withers (p.124)
- Teach the horse how to lower his head (p.98)
- Try the exercises for releasing tension in the neck (pp.112–121)
- Slow the work down and lighten the pressure

With your fingers together and pointing downwards, follow the line of the groove in front of the shoulder. Watch for signs of softening and release

Rocking the withers

Although rocking the withers is used as part of the initial observations (pp.32–51), it is also a beneficial exercise, helping to release tight shoulders and withers. It also helps the horse to open up through the chest and ribcage, lengthens the stride and encourages lift through the back and hind limb engagement. It can be done while the horse is standing still or in hand as he is moving.

> **This bodywork exercise helps...**
> - The horse to stand still
> - Encourage controlled forward movement in a horse that has become stuck or gone into freeze (p.18)
> - Teach the horse to transfer his weight from side to side
> - Encourage the horse to weight his limbs more evenly

- Place one hand, palm down, over the horse's withers, cupping the highest point. Place one foot in front of the other and keep your hips and knees soft. Keeping an even connection through your arm and hand, transfer your weight slowly onto your front foot. This will send the withers away from you. Pause for a moment and then slowly transfer your weight onto your back foot. This will bring the withers towards you. Repeat this a few times. Note whether one side is freer than the other and pay attention to how your horse reorganizes himself during this exercise.

Cup the withers at their highest point and send them away, pause, and then bring them towards you

> **My horse doesn't like rocking the withers**
> - Place the flat of your right hand on the shoulder and think about asking the horse to move slightly away from you. Support the shoulder and think about gradually releasing the shoulder to allow him to move back slowly towards you
> - Ask him to do the exercise on the move
> - Try shoulder delineation (p.123) to release the base of his neck
> - Walk him over raised poles (opposite) to encourage the withers to lift and release

Harley – Part Two

Continued from p.47. Headshy horses often have discomfort in the oral cavity. Harley was concerned about having his mouth handled, and examination revealed he had a lump on the side of his jaw. X-rays showed an old abscess and dental technician Charlie Pickman carried out thorough dental work under sedation, removing sharp teeth edges that had lacerated the sides of his tongue and cheeks.

When concerned Harley would throw his head in the air

Harley had a bloated abdomen and was tight and braced through the neck. His feet were out of balance, which was hardly surprising as he was so difficult to

Holistic vet Nick Thompson treated Harley with a photonic torch as he was too sensitive for acupuncture

shoe. Added to this he had a conformational twist in the front limbs and was very straight through the hind legs. He had heat over the right hip and was tight through the back.

A wand was used to stroke Harley over his body and down his lower legs, so that we could work towards being able to improve his foot balance. Initiating contact this way is less invasive and less threatening to the majority of horses, and within a few days Harley began to move towards people entering his stable instead of turning away to hide in the corner. Groundwork and bodywork helped him to become more comfortable through the body and his neck began to lower and lengthen. When concerned or unsure Harley would plant himself and raise his head in the air. Sometimes he would go into freeze. By moving his head a little or rocking his withers we asked him to continue in a calm and focused manner.

Pro-balance probiotics were added to Harley's feed and holistic vet Nick Thompson was called in to treat him with acupuncture and homeopathy. As he was still concerned about contact from a newcomer, Nick used a photonic torch to stimulate acupuncture points all over his body instead of needles. Photonic therapy was developed by Australian vet Brian McClaren (see p.151 for website address). It can be used to diagnose and treat a number of symptoms and blends well with all the work that we do. Nick has become a valuable part of the team at Tilley Farm.

The acupuncture points that prompted a reaction in Harley during Nick's assessment confirmed everything we had found in our initial exploration – he found problems with the front limbs, the gut, the hips, hocks and stifles (with greater sensitivity on the right side) and soft tissue discomfort through the back. After treating Harley with the photonic torch, Nick gave him the homeopathic remedy sulphur, which has a 'clearing' quality. As it helps to get things moving, it can be a very beneficial in horses that tend to become rooted when being led or under saddle.

An elastic bandage was wrapped around the end of a wand and this was used to stroke Harley down the lower legs. He was also led over different surfaces and within four days of his arrival in the yard my wonderful farrier, Tigger Barnes, was able to balance his feet and re-shoe him without any concern. Harley went from strength to strength and improved on so many levels. He would have benefited from a longer rehabilitation to develop more muscle but sadly it isn't always economically viable or practical for owners to continue with the necessary work and Harley was sold shortly after returning home.

Raised Poles

When a horse lifts a front leg over a pole, the neck should lower and the withers and shoulders should lift and release. The exception to this is if the horse is tight through the neck, shoulders or back. Walking a horse in hand over raised poles can help him release and connect through the neck and back.

> **This groundwork exercise helps...**
> - Teach engagement
> - Horses that work in a high-headed frame
> - Horses that are easily distracted
> - Loading problems
> - Transitions

- You need a minimum of two poles and four blocks or two cavalettis. The distance between the poles can be geared to the individual stride of each horse. If possible, ask someone to watch you work or teach someone how to do the exercise so that you can make observations as to how the horse is organizing himself over the poles.

- Attach the TTEAM line as described on p.100 or clip your lead rope onto the side of the headcollar. Take the end of the lead rope and the wand in the outside hand and place your other hand on the line near the headcollar. Position yourself a little in front of the horse's nose to encourage straightness and even movement through the forequarters.

- Lead your horse up to the poles and halt a couple of strides in front of the first pole. Stroke down the horse's chest and front legs with the wand, then ask your horse forward over the poles with a slight ask-and-release signal on the line. As you ask, slide your hand down the line away from the headcollar to give the horse more freedom through the neck and the head as he walks over the poles. Make a forward movement with the wand. Look in the direction in which you are going and try to feel through the lead line how the horse is organizing his body. Is his head heavy in your hand? Is there a lot of up and down movement through his neck and head? Is he pulling in one direction? Some horses will initially lift their head, trip over the poles, lift one limb higher than the others, catch each pole with the same limb or scramble their way awkwardly through the exercise but generally in a very short space of time the movements become fluid, the neck releases and the withers really free and lift.

Slide away from the headcollar as you work over the poles to give the horse freedom through the neck

My horse doesn't like raised poles

Introduce the work gradually by:
- Starting with one pole flat on the ground
- Adding more poles one by one so that you end up with a row of four poles flat on the ground
- Raising the ends of the poles one at a time

Shoulder presses in hand

This is a Connected Riding exercise that enables the horse to release the shoulder and base of the neck while supporting him through the movement. It helps him to bend and release through the ribcage and reduces any one-sided tendencies.

This groundwork exercise helps...
- Improve gait irregularities
- Hind limb engagement
- Establish lateral movement
- Lengthen and release the back
- Horses that spook and spin

- Start by working from the left side as this is likely to be easier for the horse. Stand near the shoulder, facing the side of the horse and hold the lead line up by the headcollar in your left hand. Make a soft fist with your right hand and place it in the fleshy muscle in the middle

of the shoulder – approximately two to three fist widths back from the point of the shoulder, depending on the size of the horse.

- Place your feet slightly apart with your right foot slightly forward. Slowly press your right fist into the shoulder, and slowly rotate your body to the left. Keep your knees and hips soft. Rotating your body to the left helps you to give a supportive movement through the horse's shoulder as opposed to simply pushing him over. You want him to release into the movement not push back into your hand. Hold this position for a moment and watch the horse's reaction. Slowly rotate your body back to the right and release the pressure on the shoulder. It is the release that is the most important part of the exercise as this gives the horse the opportunity to respond to the movement and to soften and adjust his posture. Pay attention to your left hand and remember to think up with the hand. This helps you to keep the contact light and connected and minimizes the chances of you

Hold the lead line by the headcollar. Make a soft fist with the other hand and place it in the fleshy part of the shoulder. Press your right fist into the shoulder by rotating to the left. Watch for signs of release

inadvertently pulling the horse's head down. Thinking 'up' doesn't mean you need to actually lift your hand. Repeat this exercise a few times and then switch to the other side. Note whether the horse is more accepting of the shoulder presses on a particular side and whether the amount of release is equal on both sides.

■ This exercise can also be done in walk. Angle your body to allow you to walk along side the horse without being trodden on. Remember to rotate your body slightly away from the horse to initiate the press. You can also try this exercise with two lead lines on the horse and take a contact on the outside rein with the hand doing the presses on the shoulder.

You can do this exercise in walk with two lines

My horse doesn't like shoulder presses in hand

- Make sure your fist is in the soft, fleshy part of the shoulder
- Dramatically reduce the pressure of the press so that the movement is minimal
- Check that you aren't pulling his head down or round with the left hand
- Try the exercises for releasing the neck (pp.112–121)
- Try rocking the withers (p.124)

Shoulder presses under saddle

You can also do the shoulder presses under saddle. Doing this exercise from the ground with the horse under saddle teaches him to soften and lengthen into the rein contact and helps him to soften and yield through his entire body.

This ridden exercise helps...

- Establish even rein contact
- Horses that draw back and work above or below the bit
- Horses that lean on the bit
- Horses that spook
- Horses that drop a shoulder
- Teach the horse to lift and work up through the withers and back
- Encourage hind limb engagement

■ Stand by the horse's shoulder to start and make a soft fist with your hand. Place your fist into the soft and fleshy part of the shoulder. You will be walking beside the horse but the principles are the same as the shoulder presses in hand. You do not need to take the rein from the rider but sometimes, and only if it is safe to do, it can be helpful, particularly if the horse has a habit of drawing his neck back and working behind the vertical.

Shoulder presses under saddle help the hindquarters to engage

My horse doesn't like shoulder presses under saddle

Work through the checklist for shoulder presses in hand (left) and check the following:
- Saddle fit
- Bit and bridle fit
- Rider posture
- Teeth

Balance rein

The TTEAM balance rein looks a little like a neckstrap but the part of this ingenious piece of equipment that makes contact with the horse is made of rope 9mm (³/₈in) in diameter. It is also longer than a neckstrap to enable the rider to use the balance rein in conjunction with the snaffle rein.

The balance rein is a simple and highly effective tool that is helpful for rounding, steadying, straightening and balancing the horse. It is useful for horses that brace and shorten through the neck, shoulders and back and can reduce pulling, napping and spooking as tension through the neck, shoulders and back is greatly diminished.

The balance rein is excellent for horses that are above the vertical or for those that spook...

This ridden exercise helps...

- Horses that jig
- Horses that drop a shoulder or spin
- Teach riders to balance through their body instead of their hands
- Improve rider posture
- High-headed horses
- Nervous horses
- Horses that snatch, lean on, or take hold of the bit
- Start young horses under saddle
- Improve focus
- Horses that rush fences when jumping

...or rush, and the effects are usually instantaneous

- You don't need to purchase a balance rein for this exercise as you can easily braid your own from a length of climbing rope. However, you do need to ensure that your rope cannot become loose and fall off.

- The easiest way to hold the balance rein is to take the bridle rein between the little finger and ring finger and the balance rein between the ring and middle fingers. Another way is to hold the balance rein between the ring finger and little finger and the bridle rein on the outside of the little finger.

- Taking the balance rein in both hands, ask your horse to walk forward for a few steps. Give a gentle ask-and-release signal on the balance rein to steady the horse or to halt. When the rope makes contact with the base of the neck the horse is encouraged to soften and lengthen his neck. You may need to experiment a few times before he understands what is being asked of him. Ensure your reins are not too short as this will inhibit his ability to release his withers and neck.

Take the bridle rein between the little finger and ring finger and the balance rein between the ring and little finger

My horse doesn't like the balance rein

- Check the saddle fit
- Ensure you aren't pulling on the balance rein. You need to ask and release otherwise the horse will simply lean into the contact and become sore through the base of the neck and shoulders
- If your horse is extremely tight through the base of the neck and has been habitually on the forehand, he may not feel the ask and release signal initially. Try introducing the balance rein from the ground (see opposite)

■ To introduce the balance rein in hand, you will need someone to lead your horse while you work with the balance rein or rope. They must stay up by the horse's nose, otherwise you will fall over each other. Undo the balance rein, so that you can remove it quickly if necessary, and place it round the base of the horse's neck. If you are on the horse's left side, hold the balance rein in your left hand to give the signal while your right hand supports the other end of the rope.

■ Ask the horse to walk for a few paces and then ask for a 'Whoooa'. Give a slow ask-and-release signal on the rope or balance rein and keep repeating the signal until the horse stops. Remember that it is on the release that the horse will re-balance and therefore be able to halt. The person leading can give a signal with the lead line and wand to help the horse to understand what is being asked of him. When you give the 'ask' signal with the left hand, take the rope up the line of the shoulder.

To achieve and maintain a well muscled back...

■ Warm up thoroughly
■ Build a solid basic foundation and increase the difficulty of exercises gradually
■ Avoid or reduce tension through bodywork and groundwork and exercises under saddle
■ Allow the horse to walk on a loose rein and stretch at frequent intervals during ridden work
■ Ensure the saddle is fitting correctly and is not placing pressure on the vulnerable loin area
■ Ensure teeth and feet are balanced, in good health and receive appropriate and regular attention
■ Ensure the horse isn't pushed beyond his capability or forced into an outline
■ Cool down thoroughly
■ Leave the saddlecloth or pad on for a short while after work to prevent the warmed back muscles cooling too quickly
■ Wash off with warm water

If your horse is concerned or overly sensitive through the base of the neck, introduce the balance rein from the ground

Withers, back and hindquarters

Movement between the thoracic vertebrae is more limited than in the cervical vertebrae in the neck. The strength of the back comes from a combination of ligaments, tendons, muscles and bones. Exercises aimed at strengthening the back and facilitating engagement of the hindquarters are vital to minimize the risk of injury.

Allow the horse to walk on a loose rein and stretch during ridden work

Free up your horse

TTouches

You can use Clouded Leopard TTouches (p.94) all over the horse's body. Use them on the neck, back, hindquarters and down either side of the tail to increase circulation, suppleness and performance. TTouches will reduce stress and connect the horse through the entire body.

You can use the Clouded Leopard TTouch all over the horse's body

> **My horse doesn't like Clouded Leopard TTouches**
> Keep your hand soft, your wrist straight and remember to breathe. Try:
> - Doing the TTouch with the back of your hand
> - Lightening the contact
> - Altering the direction of the circle
> - Starting with a half circle
> - Slowing down or speeding up the circle
> - Finding a place where the circle is acceptable and work back towards the area that was giving him cause for concern

Tail work

As a non-habitual movement, tail work gives the horse's nervous system a new experience and encourages the horse to relax through the entire body. Tail work can help connect the horse from his head through the body to the end of the dock. It can release tension in the back, neck and poll, increase flexibility, improve balance and encourage engagement of the hindquarters.

> **These bodywork exercises help...**
> - Assist recovery of endurance or event horses
> - Overcome stress and fatigue
> - Horses that are nervous in traffic or noise-sensitive
> - Horses that lack engagement
> - Loading problems

Circles Circling the tail can help the horse to release tight back muscles and reduce tension in the back and hindquarters. This is an excellent and effective exercise for ridden horses and those that are stabled for long hours or on box rest.

Circling the tail helps to release the back and can be done once the horse is under saddle to help improve engagement

- Although it is described as though you are working from the left, you can carry out this exercise from either side. Facing the side of the tail, put your left hand under the dock a few inches from the top. Hold the tail further down with your right hand and make a gentle arch in the tail by lifting with your left hand and pushing slightly in with your right. If the tail is supple the shape will resemble a question mark. If the tail is stiff it may not flex and must not be forced into a shape.

- Circle the tail gently in both directions. As you make the circles, think of the movement coming through your body and shoulders rather than just your arms. Softening your knees will help keep the movement relaxed. The size of the circles will depend on the tightness of the tail.

A supple tail will resemble a question mark

If the tail is clamped take a handful of hair and circle in both directions

Hold the tail and apply slight traction with a gentle and steady feel

Always keep the circles within a range of motion that is comfortable for the horse. If the tail is clamped, take a handful of hair a third of the way down the dock and circle both directions. Holding the hair, apply tension backwards, pause for a moment and then release and slowly follow the movement forwards.

Weighting the tail Stand behind the horse with your feet shoulder width apart. Place one foot forward and the other back. Hold the tail and gradually apply traction to it with a gentle and steady feel, transferring your weight from the front to the back foot. Hold the traction for about five seconds and then release slowly and smoothly. Keep the tailbone in alignment with the horse's spine and make the release slow to avoid a domino effect on the vertebrae. If the horse starts to move or walk away use less pressure or go back to moving the tail in circles. If your horse has a loose or floppy tail, push the tail gently towards the horse's body rather than applying traction.

Please note
Only stand behind your horse if it is safe to do so.

My horse doesn't like tail work
Go back to something that he enjoyed. Try:
- Clouded Leopard TTouches (p.94) around the hindquarters and down the hindlegs
- Using the wand to stroke the horse all over his body, including down the hindlegs and tail
- Standing at the side of the horse and gently stroking strands of hair without lifting the tail from the tail groove
- Standing at the side and taking the hair at the top of the tail then gently rocking the tail slowly from side to side to release it at the top of the dock
- Doing circular TTouches down either side of the dock – this should trigger the tail to lift slightly from the tail groove
- Hindleg circles (below)
- Forelock pulls (p.115)
- Having someone work the ears (p.104) while you start working around the hindquarter
- Mouth work (p.89) – nervous horses are often tight in both the mouth and the tail
- Other exercises for the back and hindquarters and belly lifts (p.136) to release tension through the back

Hindleg circles

Moving a horse's hindlegs in small clockwise and anti-clockwise circles loosens stiff hindquarters. It is a quick and easy way of helping horses that are stabled for long hours during the winter and elderly horses that stiffen up in colder weather. Leg circles can be done when the hooves are picked out. You may find that the horse can circle one leg more easily than the other, is reluctant to pick up one leg or is significantly stiffer on one side. Horses that find it hard to engage will often have reduced mobility in the hindlegs. In just a few days this simple exercise will improve the horse's performance under saddle.

> **This bodywork exercise helps...**
> - A horse to release through the back
> - Increase circulation to the limbs

- If you are standing on the right, support the hindleg by holding the hind cannon bone in your right hand while supporting the hoof in your left hand. Rest your left elbow on your left knee or thigh to prevent tension in your back. Ensure your feet are in a position that enables you to stand in balance and away from the hoof in case the leg is snatched back and stamped down. Circle your body slowly to get the movement through the horse's limb. Keep the range of movement small – taking the leg as far as it will go will cause more tension.

Support the hind cannon with your inside hand and cradle the hoof in the outside hand

- It is important to make the circles under the horse as opposed to taking the leg out to the side.

> **My horse doesn't like hindleg circles**
> - Stroke him all over with the wand including the hind limbs and hooves
> - Simplify the exercise and ask him to lift each leg in turn without trying to hold the leg
> - Have someone stroke the diagonal leg or other hind leg with a wand
> - Try asking him to lift the leg and hold it gently but supportively for a few moments before putting it back to the ground.
> - Try picking up the leg from the opposite side
> - Try circling the front legs first (p.122)
> - Do tail work (pp.130 & 138)
> - Teach him to back up in hand
> - Walk him over different surfaces
> - Follow the other exercises for the back and hindquarters
> - Try hindleg circles with the horse standing between two poles to help him balance

The labyrinth

The principle of the labyrinth exercise is to help the horse become less one-sided, more supple and co-ordinated, and to use his hindquarters more effectively. The aim is to teach the horse to walk slowly through the pattern of poles, stopping before each turn. Horses that are out of balance will have a tendency to rush through the exercise. By holding a wand in your outside hand you can give a signal to the horse to move forward and to halt. This exercise is used a lot by the Thoroughbred Rehabilitation Centre in the United Kingdom as it has a very relaxing effect on the ex-racehorses. It is perfect for owners who have limited time and for horses that are on restricted work. It can be done, alone or with a helper, in a field or a manège or even laid on the track to the field enabling you to work your horse through the labyrinth as you turn him out and bring him in from the field.

> **This groundwork exercise helps horses that...**
> - Spook
> - Are concerned over poles or road markings
> - Rush through narrow spaces
> - Are easily distracted
> - Crowd their handler

■ The labyrinth is a pattern of six 4m (12ft) poles laid as shown (left). The width between the poles can vary, depending on the size and balance of your horse – initially try placing them approximately 1.2m (4ft) apart.

■ If you are working alone, start by leading the horse from the near side, as you and he will probably find this easier. If he is out of balance and crowds the handler use the homing pigeon (p.116). Lead the horse slowly through the labyrinth halting before each turn. Make sure you stay up in front of his nose. While the horse is moving forward, use the wand(s) as an extension of the arm to guide the horse through the labyrinth. You may need to step outside the labyrinth to allow your horse room to turn. To prepare for a transition to halt give a gentle ask-and-release signal on the line and bring the wand back towards the horse's chest. Use your voice and, as you say 'Whoooaa', reach across the chest with the wand and touch the point of the opposite shoulder. This encourages the horse to keep his hindquarters straight while stopping. Stroke down the underside of the neck and down the chest and forelegs with the wand to help your horse balance in halt and stay relaxed.

■ If your horse cannot stop when you first ask him, or is concerned about standing between poles, lead him out over the poles and try again. To walk give a gentle forward ask-and-release signal on the lead line and move the wand forward to indicate the direction in which you want him to move. Use your voice to ask for walk and allow him time to process the information. He has to hear the command, understand it and then respond to the request.

■ Lead the horse through the labyrinth from both directions. Note how he negotiates the corners. If he finds it difficult to engage behind or has poor balance he may initially get his hind legs 'stuck' behind the pole. He may shuffle his hind legs together instead of crossing one in front of the other as he bends around the end of the pole and may find it easy to turn in one direction but not the other. Precision is the key and care must be taken not to rush or overwork him.

The labyrinth improves concentration and settles horses in a very short space of time

■ Ground exercises can be physically and mentally tiring for all concerned – several short sessions are often more effective than one long session. To keep the horse's interest, use the labyrinth in a number of different ways. Walk over the poles or stop in the labyrinth and do some TTouch work. If you have had trouble getting him

You can also use the labyrinth as walk-over poles

to relax with the TTouches in his stable, going through the labyrinth a few times may help him to settle and concentrate better. He may also find it easier to stand in balance with the poles on either side of him as a visual aid.

Other benefits of the labyrinth

The labyrinth can highlight any concerns your horse may have. Working youngsters or rehabilitating horses in hand through the labyrinth wearing a saddle allows them to experience the feeling of the saddle in a totally different way. Any item of tack that we put on our horses changes their balance. It can sometimes be the case that, even though it may seem that the horse has completely accepted the saddle, he freezes or gets stuck when asked to move through the labyrinth with the saddle on, even if he could move easily through the labyrinth prior to being tacked up.

My horse doesn't like the labyrinth

■ Start with two parallel poles wide apart and walk your horse through them
■ Next, repeat the exercise and ask your horse to stop in the middle of the poles
■ Ask him to turn left or right out of the poles so that he has to bend around the top of the pole
■ Try the zigzag exercise (p.111)
■ Open up the labyrinth so that there are less turns and more space

Hindquarter and loin presses

Hindquarter and loin presses follow the same principles as the shoulder presses (see pp.126–127). They activate the hind end of the horse and teach him how to soften and yield through the body.

This ridden exercise helps...

■ Horses to track up
■ Lateral work
■ Improve gait irregularities
■ Improve balance and co-ordination

■ If you are the person on the ground, start on the left side of the horse, as this is likely to be more acceptable to him. Keep to the inside and place your right hand on the loin area. Check your posture, and as the horse is walking send his loins away from you for a few strides by pushing gently up and away with the right hand.

Do presses at various points on the ribcage

- Maintain the contact and slowly release the pressure keeping the connection through your hand and body. As you release you should feel a surge of power under your hand and the horse's stride should lengthen. The rider should feel the same surge and also elevation through the horse's back. Repeat this a few times and switch reins to work the other side. You can also do this exercise by pressing on the hip or on various points on the ribcage.

Stand on the left side. Place your right hand on the top of the dock and your left hand on the upper side of the ribcage

Ribs, belly and flank

Many horses carry tension through the ribs, belly and flank. Although this is often linked to tension in the back, it can also arise from accidents such as falling over or getting caught when going through stable doors, gateways or when travelling. Other contributory factors include stress, an overtight girth, roller or surcingle and/or poor saddle fit. Releasing tension through the barrel will improve balance, lateral work, digestion and encourage deep rhythmical breathing.

Rib releases

Rib releases increase mobility through the barrel and back. They reduce stiffness and help the horse to be less one-sided.

- Stand on the left side of the horse with your feet apart. Place your right hand on the top of the dock and your left hand on the upper side of the horse's ribcage just behind the shoulder. Slowly rotate your body to the right. This will draw the horse's hindquarter towards you as your left hand sends the ribs slightly away from you. Hold this position for a moment and then slowly rotate back to the left. The release is the important part of the exercise. Gradually moving your left hand along the ribcage, work slowly towards the last ribs. Repeat on the other side.

- Keep the movement small. If you try to ask for too much bend the horse will step away from you. Note whether he find it easier on a particular side or whether there are places on his ribs that feel 'stuck'.

Belly lifts

Belly lifts help horses to release through the ribs, belly and back. They are useful as a step prior to introducing a surcingle, roller or girth and can be helpful for horses that are over-sensitive to the rider's leg.

> **This bodywork exercise helps...**
> - Encourage deep breathing
> - Promote relaxation
> - Horses that hold their breath or blow out their bellies when girthed

- You will need a long stretchy length of bandage, such as an exercise bandage. You can do this exercise alone or with another person. If your horse is sensitive to contact on the belly you will need someone to hold his head.

- Pass the bandage under the belly, bringing the ends up to the top of the back. Start the lifts on the girth area. If you are working alone, support one end of the bandage near the spine and gently lift the other end (the one nearest you) for a count of four. Hold the bandage in place for another count of four and then slowly release for a count of eight. The release is the important part of the exercise. Avoid pulling the bandage tight – the exercise is more effective if you simply make contact with the horse's ribs and belly rather than pulling all the stretch from the bandage. If you have another person holding the other side of the bandage, experiment by releasing alternately as well as simultaneously.

- Move the bandage back about 5cm (2in) or so with both hands and repeat. Continue as far back as you can and watch the horse for any signs of concern.

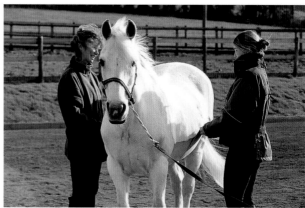

Try releasing the bandage alternately as well as simultaneously

Allowing the horse to turn to watch what you are doing reduces concern

> **My horse doesn't like belly lifts**
> - Hold the bandage in place without lifting
> - Slow the movement down
> - Stand on the other side of the horse if you are working alone

Start by lifting around the girth area and watch for signs of release

Work as far back as is comfortable for the horse

The star

This TTEAM exercise teaches the horse to open and flex through the ribs. It encourages him to lower his neck and lift his back and to step through with the hindlegs.

> **This groundwork exercise helps...**
> - Horses that are stiff
> - Horses that trail their quarters or fall through the shoulder
> - Teach a horse to soften and yield through the body
> - Improve hoof–eye co-ordination

- Lay the poles in a fan shape with one end raised on a block. Lead the horse over the poles at their lowest point. Stay up by the horse's head and use your wand to show him where you want him to go. You can then advance the exercise by asking him to walk over the middle of the poles while you are walking one pole ahead. Lead him from both sides and in both directions.

Lead the horse over the poles at their lowest point

Work in both directions

> **My horse doesn't like the star**
> - Lay the poles flat on the ground
> - Reduce the number of poles
> - Walk the 'S' (p.118) to free him through the neck and back
> - Work through the zigzag poles (p.111) and labyrinth (p.132)
> - Check your leading position and posture

Pelvic rotations

Learning to rotate your hips can really help your horse under saddle. It will also help you to alter several of your own habits, such as dropping a hip or a shoulder. This ridden exercise, which is part of the Connected Riding technique, has an incredibly powerful effect on the horse.

> **This ridden exercise helps...**
> - Free a horse through his barrel and spine
> - Improve a horse's balance and co-ordination
> - Enable a horse to release from the poll right through to the hindquarters

- Find neutral pelvis (see p.86). Now do a little swivelling motion slowly from side to side. Ensure that you are rotating from the pelvis and not simply twisting through the upper body. If the motion comes from your hips, your legs will move slightly as you swivel. If you are twisting from the upper body, the movement will not influence your legs. Swivel left to help your horse through a left turn and swivel right to help your horse on a right bend. If your horse braces and rushes, try alternate swivels left and right to help him relax and soften.

> **My horse doesn't like pelvic rotations**
> Check your posture and:
> - Pay attention to your wrists and hands and avoid pulling the horse into the movement with the rein
> - Make the movement smaller
> - Remember to float forward (p.89) with each stride
> - Do walking the 'S' (p.118) with the horse before mounting

Tail

The tail is another area of the horse's body that receives very little attention, yet it can influence the way the horse moves through the entire body.

Tail work

Tail work reduces fearful responses in horses and can improve hind limb action. It is also beneficial for horses that kick, BUT extreme caution should be taken when introducing it. If in any doubt – don't attempt it.

Hair slides and purling are simple ways to work on the horse's tail (for more tail exercises see p.130).

> **This bodywork exercise helps...**
> - Calm a nervous horse
> - Prepare a horse to have his tail handled
> - Prepare a mare for breeding

Hair slides Stand to one side of the horse facing the side of the tail. If you are on the horse's left side, place your left hand on his hip or hindquarter and gently stroke strands of hair with fingers of the other hand. This settles the horse and is a good way to introduce tail work.

- Once your horse is happy, you can move behind him. Stand with your feet apart and take the hair on either side of the tail at the top of the dock in both hands. Stroke the hair in alternate moves transferring your weight from one foot to the other with each move. If your horse has a pulled tail you will not be able to do this exercise so effectively.

Purling is an exercise that softens the tail. It improves lateral work, co-ordination, engagement and balance. Stand behind the horse and support the tail under the dock with both hands, keeping your thumbs on top of the tail. Feel the vertebrae with your fingers. Slowly and very, very gently flex the tail slightly up and down between the vertebrae using your fingers and thumbs to create the movement. Work from the top of the tail down to the end of the tailbone and note if the quality of movement changes as you work down the tail.

Supporting the tail under the dock, keeping your thumbs on top...

...flex it gently up and down between the vertebrae

> **My horse doesn't like tail work**
> - Stroke the horse's back, belly and hindquarters with the wand
> - Use the wand to stroke the tail and to lift strands of tail hair until the horse is more relaxed
> - Use the Clouded Leopard TTouch (p.94) on the back, hindquarters and on the top of the dock
> - Take your time. It can sometimes take several sessions to release a tight tail
> - If the horse becomes concerned at any point go back to where he accepted the contact and work slowly towards the area that is causing concern

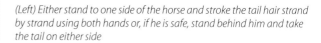

(Left) Either stand to one side of the horse and stroke the tail hair strand by strand using both hands or, if he is safe, stand behind him and take the tail on either side

Legs

Increasing circulation and movement in the legs can help reduce the risk of injury and will improve your horse's balance and therefore performance. Accustoming your horse to having his legs handled on a regular basis enables you to check for injuries or small changes and apply any necessary treatments more easily.

Python lifts

This TTEAM exercise increases circulation, encourages more even weight distribution through the limbs and can help horses that have concerns about having their legs handled.

> **This bodywork exercise helps...**
> - Horses that stumble and trip
> - Filled legs
> - Nervous horses
> - Horses become accustomed to the farrier
> - Horses that have spent a long time travelling or being stabled

- Place both hands on either side of the leg and using enough pressure to support the tissue, gently move the skin slowly upwards. Do not force the movement nor lift the skin as high as it will go. Pause for four seconds and slowly glide the skin back down to where you started, taking twice as long on the downward movement as you did on the upward motion.

- Slide your hands over the surface of the skin down the leg approximately 5cm (2in) and repeat the exercise. Continue down the leg as far as is possible. If you are unsure about how your horse will respond, remain standing rather than squatting. If you do squat, stay on the balls of your feet so that you remain in balance and can move quickly if necessary. With a quiet horse, work the leg from the top all the way down to the fetlock. You can also use this lifting movement of the skin on other parts of the horse's body by moving the skin upwards and gently guiding it back down again with the palm of one hand.

Python lifts help to improve circulation to the hoof

Place both hands on either side of the leg

Work down to the fetlock and finish by holding the fetlock joint for a moment

Free up your horse

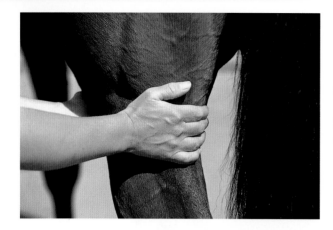

My horse doesn't like python lifts
- Do Clouded Leopard TTouches (p.94) down the limbs
- Stroke the limbs with the wand (see opposite)
- Stroke down the leg with the back of your hand
- Move the skin upwards with one hand rather than both

When working on the hind limbs, start as high up the leg as possible

Jack – Part Two

Jack's bizarre type of wind-sucking is probably linked to the damage done to his poll when a tractor was used to drag him into a trailer

Continued from p.53. Tina constance, my assistant, and I wanted to primarily focus on bodywork with Jack, so we showed Michelle ear work (p.104) to reduce stress and python lifts down the underside of the neck to help release the tension that Jack inevitably held in this area. A vet check had not been able to come up with a resolution to Jack's problems, so even if there was an ongoing physical problem in the throat, the work would definitely help him.

By doing TTouch work on the upper part of the neck Michelle gave Jack a new experience. When work was done around the poll Jack would draw in his tongue. He found it incredibly hard to stand so we did a little groundwork as well and incorporated tail work (pp.130 & 138) and other TTouches into the session to help him become more connected through the body. We were also able to fit him with a wider saddle to help him develop better muscling through the back. When Jack went back to his paddock there was already a significant change. He did not go straight to the rails and start his strange behaviour. In fact he barely did it all. Each time he looked as though he was going to start Michelle walked up to him and did more python lifts down the underside of his neck.

We returned to Cyprus the following year to run a three-day riding clinic with trainer, instructor and dressage rider Dan Hammond. I was pleased to see that Michelle had signed up for the course and asked her what had happened to the horse with the strange behaviour – I had looked quickly around the corrals on our arrival but couldn't see him. Michelle pointed to a smart little bay with a bright eye that was standing quietly by the rails on his own. Jack was totally unrecognizable. His body shape had changed, his back had filled out and he was relaxed. So relaxed in fact he was almost asleep. Michelle told me that the changes were not only physical. Jack could now happily be left alone, could stand tied up without getting distressed and could be taken up to the yard to be saddled. Above all he only did his strange behaviour immediately after eating and even then would only do it for a few moments. Yes he still pokes his tongue out when ridden and his head and front limbs do move rather strangely if you pay close attention to his action but he is happy, forward going and enjoying his life.

Michelle and the team at Episkopi have done incredible work with Jack. It was so good to see him again and so refreshing to know that even in a country where the opportunity for change is somewhat limited, this work can make a lasting difference.

Stroking with the wand

A lot of horses that appear to be whip-shy are generally found to be lacking in spatial awareness and are often concerned about objects on the ground or carried by the wind. By stroking their legs with the wand, you can help them to be more connected through the body, more grounded and more focused. This exercise also helps to settle and quieten nervous horses.

> ### This bodywork exercise helps...
> - Horses to stand
> - Encourage more effective movement
> - Horses that stumble or trip
> - Horse that habitually touch a pole with the same hoof
> - Horses to overcome concerns about being touched
> - Sensory integration (see p.14)

...and his hind limbs

Stroking the legs with the wand helps to settle a horse and accustoms him to contact on both his front limbs...

- Take the lead line or rope in one hand and the wand in the other. Stroke the horse's chest with the wand a few times and continue down the front legs. Stroke under the belly and if the horse is calm stroke the hindlegs. Let the movement come from your feet and refrain from tightening your grip around the wand. If you lock your body or fingers it may feel uncomfortable for the horse. Stroke firmly enough to produce a slight bend in the wand. If the contact is to light it may tickle the horse. Watch the horse's reactions at all times and remember to breathe. Make sure he is not in freeze (p.18). If he is worried, go back to stroking him where he was comfortable and work slowly towards the area that concerned him.

> ### My horse doesn't like being stroked with the wand
> - Turn the wand around so that it appears shorter
> - Use a smaller riding crop at first or even a small piece of wood
> - Experiment with stroking him in other areas before stroking down the limbs

Poles in hand

Teaching your horse to negotiate any pattern of poles helps to develop a more even and balanced gait. To really fine-tune your horse's ability to co-ordinate his limbs you can teach him to step over a pole one leg at a time.

This groundwork exercise helps...
- Teach a horse to stand square
- Focus
- Nervous horses
- Encourage lightness and engagement
- Develop precision in both the horse and handler
- Alter habitual patterns of moving

- It is beneficial to teach this exercise to the horse working from both sides. You will be subtler with the signal on the horse's head, and therefore more successful, if you use the TTEAM lead line.

- Halt your horse in front of one pole laid on the ground. Ask him to step over the pole using the wand to draw him forward. As he lifts his other front leg over the pole bring the wand towards his chest and rotate your body a quarter turn towards him so that he stops with his front legs one side of the pole. If he can do this part of the exercise easily, ask him to walk on and bring his hind limbs over the pole. Next time halt again in front of the pole and ask him to bring one front leg over the pole. Give a light signal with the wand and with the lead line to move and to halt. You can then ask him to take the leg back over the pole or bring the second leg forward. Repeat this exercise with the hind limbs.

- Note whether the horse lifts the same leg first each time and try to change this pattern if possible. Stroking down the leg you want him to move and tapping the relevant hooves will help him understand what you are asking him to do. Precision is the key to success and it can take time for both the horse and the handler to perfect this exercise.

My horse doesn't like working with the pole
- Teach him to walk over a single pole without stopping
- Keep the lesson short and intersperse it with other pole work
- Teach him to move each leg one at a time without the pole
- Make sure you aren't pulling or dragging him off balance

Halt your horse in front of the pole

Ask him to step over the pole and to halt with it between the fore and hind legs

Ask him to step one front leg over the pole

See if he can bring one hind leg over the pole

Hooves

Most horses are habituated to having their hooves handled only by the farrier or when their feet are picked out and horses that are nervous about having their hooves handled are often habitually in the flight reflex (see p.18).

TTouches

Doing Clouded Leopard and Racoon TTouches (pp.94–95) around the coronary band, on the hoof wall and around the sole increases a horse's awareness of his feet and teaches him not to react to contact on his hoof with a reflex action of lifting the foot. This is a useful exercise for horses that stumble or trip or for horses that are on long term box rest.

Teach him to step over the pole with the other front leg to change habitual ways of moving

Ridden poles

Riding over any combination of poles can be used to help a horse gain self-confidence and self-carriage. If your horse has never worked over ground poles before or is worried about touching poles, teach the exercises in hand first.

> **This bodywork exercise helps...**
> - Horses that are nervous
> - Prepare a youngster for the farrier
> - Accustom a horse to having his feet washed or brushed
> - Improve balance

- Start on the front limbs. Remember to stay balanced on your feet in case you have to jump out of the way. Begin by working on the left side of the horse and stroke down the lower leg with the back of your right hand so that you don't take your horse by surprise. Make one and a quarter circular movements with your fingertips all around the coronary band and hoof wall. As the skin around the coronary band will have very little elasticity and the hoof wall and sole will not move at all it is important that you roll your fingertips around to create the circular movement. You can then pick up the foot and work around the frog and sole.

Riding over and through patterns of poles improves hoof–eye co-ordination, focus and balance

TTouches around the coronary band increase awareness and work the ting points (p.72)

My horse doesn't like TTouches on the hoof

- Do the circular TTouches or python lifts (p.139) on the shoulder or hindquarter and work gradually down the limb. If your horse becomes concerned at any point go back to where the contact was acceptable and start again

- Stroke down the horse's legs with the wand then tap the hooves lightly with the button end of the wand
- Use an artist's paintbrush or clean hoof oil brush to make circular movements on the coronary band and hoof

Try circles or python lifts down the hindquarters

- Cover your hand with a glove or mitt

Different Surfaces

There are many benefits to teaching horses to walk over different surfaces. It increases levels of self-confidence and self-control, encourages more efficient brain–body use and improves hoof–eye co-ordination.

These groundwork exercises help...

- Loading problems
- Nervous horses
- Horses that lack trust
- Horses that spook at objects on the ground

These exercises are broken down into simple steps. It is not about forcing the horse over the different surface or punishing him if he cannot do as asked. Showing him how to do the exercise and making him do the exercise are two totally different things. By being patient, taking your time and really listening to the horse you can usually teach him to walk over a variety of objects quietly and safely in a few sessions.

Plastic sheeting You will need to use the TTEAM lead line and wand. Lay two sheets of plastic wide apart on the ground in an open-ended arrowhead (right) and simply walk the horse around the outside. Make sure there is no danger of the plastic moving in the wind and frightening the horse.

Harley is sensitive about having his legs handled. Contact with the back of the hand is more acceptable to horses that are worried about being touched

- Remember horses are more visually aware of change than most humans and even an everyday object in a new place can be a cause for concern. If your horse is able to walk quietly past the plastic, halt in front of it and then walk through the arrowhead.

- Repeat this step and ask him to halt on the other side. If he cannot halt it means that he still has a level of concern and is worried about having the object behind him, in which case go back a few steps. If he is unconcerned take him through again and ask him to halt between the sheets. Stroke his legs with the wand and let him look at the plastic. Continue through the arrowhead. If the horse remains calm lead him through again and this time walk over a sheet yourself to accustom him to the noise.

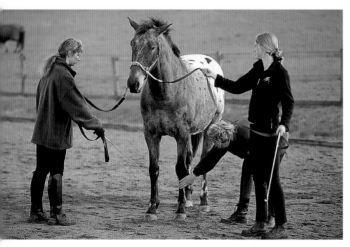

Breaking down the exercises into simple steps enables Harley to gain confidence quickly

■ Continue by narrowing the arrowhead a little and leading him through again repeating the steps. Narrow the arrowhead again until the sheets are almost touching and repeat the exercise. If he is still calm, ask the horse to walk across the plastic. Ask him to step onto the plastic and teach him to back off the sheet to begin with.

Walk the horse quietly through the arrowhead

Gradually make the arrowhead narrower

Walk on the plastic to accustom him to the noise

Walk him over the shorter side of the plastic sheet

Stroke the horse's legs with the wand during the different stages to keep him relaxed

Ask him to step onto the sheet and halt

Free up your horse

Wooden boards and matting If you want to teach your horse to walk over other surfaces start by leading him past the object and continue as for plastic sheeting. Although you will probably be working with one piece of board or matting, the principles are the same. Make sure that there is no risk of the horse cracking or breaking the board or slipping on its surface. Once he can step calmly onto a raised wooden board, you can teach him to use a low level teeter-totter (see-saw).

Horses can learn to use the teeter-totter in one session if you make each step clear and simple

Using Feed

You can use small amounts of feed, given by hand or placed on the wood, plastic or matting to help him gain more confidence. Make sure he can't grab the plastic at the same time and scare himself. It is not to be used as a lure but as a means for helping the horse learn faster. Eating also triggers the parasympathetic nervous system, which promotes a sense of calm. Don't use feed if your horse snatches and grabs at it, this may be a sign of concern.

Random Poles

This is an easy exercise to prepare, as there is no specific pattern. Vary the arrangement of the poles each time to keep your horse focused. Since the horse has to think about where he is placing his feet, the exercise helps proprioception (p.14) and co-ordination. It also helps horses to become accustomed to having objects around their hooves and teaches them to pick their way over fallen logs or debris on the ground.

This groundwork exercise helps...

- Horses that stumble and trip
- High-headed horses
- Improve confidence
- Horses that rush

- Lay a minimum of six poles in any pattern flat on the ground, varying the angles and spacing between each pole. Attach the lead line as shown on p.100 and lead your horse towards the poles. Stop in front of the poles and stroke down the horse's legs with the wand. You can tap the hooves or the poles with the wand to attract the horse's attention. Then ask him to walk forward carefully over the poles. Even the clumsiest horse will usually become lighter on his feet and more precise with his hoof placement after negotiating the poles a couple of times.

Random poles help to improve co-ordination and confidence. You can see Toto is really focused on picking his way carefully through this exercise

---

My horse doesn't like random poles

- Stroke his front and back limbs with the wand and tap each hoof in turn.
- Teach him to walk and stop with his front legs over a single pole laid on the ground
- Then teach him to stop after walking over a single pole on the ground so that his back feet are near the pole
- Once he is settled to working with a single pole add more poles one by one
- Keep the poles at a fair distance at first so that he doesn't feel trapped and gradually increase the complexity of the pattern

---

Holistic horse care

Conformation, training, development, diet and management all contribute to the health of a horse, as well as its posture. The traditional Chinese medicine approach of the need for balance between all systems for optimum wellbeing is highly appropriate, for musculoskeletal injury can easily occur if any imbalance exists within the horse. While it is very important to develop the correct muscles and a correct outline when under saddle, schooling difficulties can be improved by making changes to the way we handle and manage the horse.

By being aware of how the horse responds and reacts in the environment we have created for him, we can enhance his day-to-day existence. Time in the saddle can be spent on advancing his education rather than trying to undo tension patterns inadvertently set up throughout the day. Resistance to aids when ridden is directly linked to areas of tension in the horse's body. Simple alterations to his routine can bring big rewards and, in a relatively short space of time, he will be calmer to handle and more consistent in his behaviour and performance.

Haynets

To eat from a haynet, a horse has to alter his natural posture. Grazing horses or those that are fed hay on the floor maintain a low head and neck position while chewing. This enables the molars to occlude correctly. The body remains relatively straight and the horse will generally move around a little while he eats. Little or no excessive strain is placed on any one part of the body.

When eating from a haynet, a horse quickly settles to a habitual pattern of pulling hay from the net. His back will drop as he draws back with a mouthful of hay and his head and neck will often twist the same way each time. A horse fed in this fashion will tend to chew each mouthful holding his head and neck higher. This posture can cause or exacerbate uneven muscle development and inappropriate wear of both the incisors and the molars. It

is highly significant that the stabled horse, fed periodically throughout the day from a haynet, is more likely to develop postural, behavioural and dental problems than a horse kept in a more natural environment.

Grooming and clipping

The aim of grooming is not only to produce a shiny horse. The origins behind it are to warm and relax tight muscles and improve circulation through the whole body before and after exercise. Appropriate and sensitive grooming can aid muscle development and encourage healthy skin.

A good indicator of how a horse feels on a physical level is how he responds to being brushed. Horses that are easy to handle and able to work freely through the body are generally easy to groom. If the horse carries tension through the body, the skin will be tight and grooming will be uncomfortable for him. Even after hours of hard labour, the coat may look dull as the tightness of the skin inhibits natural oil production. The horse will fidget, bite, pin his ears or kick in a desperate bid to tell the person that the experience is causing distress. If he is punished for his behaviour, the tension will increase and any negative aspects of grooming will be reinforced. The horse may exhibit defensive behaviour as soon as anyone approaches the stable. With a horse that is sensitive about being groomed, soft rubber grooming tools, sheepskin mitts, warm towels and small, soft face brushes can be

haynets can encourage uneven dental wear'

used instead of the more traditional tools to remove dirt and increase circulation.

Bracing, tensing or being genuinely frightened when being groomed or washed can exacerbate an incorrect posture. The head will be raised and the back dropped. The tail will be clamped and the heart rate will rise. Circulation to the tips of the ears and the lower legs will be impaired. This is the exact opposite of what we try to achieve with our horses under saddle. Sympathetic preparation will produce a horse that is less reactive, more relaxed, more focused and ready and willing to work. For example, hosing down should be done with consideration and care. Hosing down with cold water and spraying water in the horse's face, particularly when facing him, can make him raise his head, drop his back and contract and tighten his muscles. A horse that already carries tension through the body will feel the cold more than a horse that is more relaxed.

Horses that are tight in the body, have ticklish areas or are noise-sensitive may also over-react to being clipped. By releasing tension through the body and by introducing the clippers slowly over several sessions, if necessary, it is possible to teach the majority of horses that clipping is not a cause for concern.

When picking out feet ensure that you do not take the limb out to the side. This is a common mistake, particularly with small ponies, and can throw the horse off balance, as well as putting stress on their shoulders or hindquarters. Teach your horse to pick up a foot by giving a little squeeze and release signal on the tendon with your fingertips rather than leaning into him and pushing him off balance. If he finds it hard to balance, ask him to pick up each foot in turn before taking hold of the limb for cleaning out the hoof (or doing anything with the limbs). If the horse is happy, circle the leg as in the leg circle exercises (pp.122 & 132). If your horse is still concerned, try asking him to lift his leg from the opposite side. This will help reduce the risk of getting injured if he kicks out, will change his expectation and will remove the chances of you inadvertently pulling the limb away from his body.

Reactive behaviour when being groomed is a sign of a sensitive horse or one that is carrying tension through the body

Soft mitts can make grooming a pleasurable experience for the horse

Rubber groomers are often far more acceptable to sensitive horses

Quick Tips to Help Your Horse

- Check that the height of everyday things in your horse's life are appropriate for his size, such as tie rings and the stable door. Attaching a horse to a ring or cross ties that are too high or stabling a small horse or pony in a box with a standard door can encourage him to develop a high head carriage and a dropped back. Similarly, a low tie ring or low stable opening can make the horse fix through the neck and poll as well as causing damage to the poll if he suddenly lifts his head.

- Select the right type of feed for the breed type and the amount and type of the work the horse is doing. Many horses are overfed and under-worked, causing all sorts of behavioural problems. Itching, restlessness, nervousness and over-reactive behaviours can be linked to feed imbalances. Some horses react strongly to feeds containing plants that have phytohormones, such as alfalfa, which can trigger excessive hormonal reactions in stallions, geldings and mares. If the horse has suffered stress, is habitually anxious or is going through changes in his feed or management a pro-biotic supplement will be of huge benefit. Like humans, horses do not all require the same amount or type of feed. Discussing your requirements with an equine nutritionist will help you to develop the appropriate feeding regime for the individual horses in your care.

- To prevent your horse placing greater strain on certain limbs when stabled ensure he is standing on a surface that is as even as possible. Pushing the bedding back from the door may mean that the stabled horse is spending the greater part of his day with his hindquarters a few inches higher than his withers.

- Keep the environment as peaceful as possible. Horses are sensitive to sound and prefer a quiet life. Persistent loud noises can cause stress levels to rise and your horse may never truly relax.

Stabling and turn-out

The stabled horse is more likely to develop unwanted habits and vices. Turn-out allows the horse to graze, play and move at will and is vital for mental and physical health. If horses have to be kept in for long periods, ad lib hay, large boxes and adaptations to the stable that allow them to touch and/or see their neighbours can go a long way to minimizing potential causes of stress. In *The Behaviour of Horses*, Dr Marthe Kiley-Worthington writes that horses stabled in this way spend 47 per cent of their time eating and 40 per cent standing; the remainder is spent in lying down and other behaviours, which include interaction with their neighbours. Horses on restricted fibre that can only see other horses over the stable door spend 15 per cent of their time eating and 65 per cent of their time standing.

Mounting

Much of how we handle horses stems from the early cavalry days when swords determined how riders led and mounted horses. As with leading, mounting from the same side every day can cause uneven muscle development. The stirrup leather will lengthen in time as the leather stretches and although this may be imperceptible to the rider, the horse will feel the difference in the rider's balance. If possible, teach your horse to be mounted from the offside, too. Take care in teaching this as horses are often so habituated to being mounted from the near side that the change could frighten even the most well-trained horse. The rider often struggles to adopt a new pattern of behaviour as much as the horse.

If mounting from the offside is not an option, swap the stirrup leathers over from time to time. When mounting avoid pulling on the cantle for support. This twists the saddle and can cause discomfort to the horse. Instead place your hand on the saddle flap on the far side to keep the saddle balanced.

Finding the time

It is unlikely that you are going to find the time to work with your horse every day. Even if you only do two or three of the exercises on pp.89–146 at the weekend you will still make a difference to your horse. You can also try incorporating some of the work into your daily routine. For example:

- Do leg circles (pp.122 & 132) when picking out feet
- Run the flat of your hand over every part of your horse's body as often as you can. This will help you spot any changes in the way he feels and highlight any areas that require a little bit of extra attention
- Walk the horse in an 'S' (p.118) when turning out, bringing in or walking to the mounting block or set up a labyrinth (p.132) that you can lead your horse through on the way to the paddock

- Use a sheepskin mitt as part of the grooming routine especially for the sensitive head and face area and move the skin in a circular movement as you go

Walk the horse in an 'S' when leading

- Remove bedding and mud from the tail with your fingers as you do hair slides (p.138)
- Do belly lifts (p.136) with the girth before tightening it

Do belly lifts with the girth before tightening

Addresses and Further Reading

TTEAM Addresses

Sarah Fisher
TTEAM UK
Tilley Farm, Farmborough
Bath, England BA2 0AB
www.ttouchtteam.co.uk

Robyn Hood
TTEAM Canada
5435 Rochdell Rd
Vernon, Canada, BC V1B 3E8
www.icefarm.shaw.ca

Linda Tellington Jones
TTEAM USA
PO Box 3793, Santa Fe,
USA, NM 87501
www.lindatellingtonjones.com

Log on to the US website for contact details for TTEAM around the world

Other Useful Addresses

Association of Chartered Physiotherapists in Animal Therapy (ACPAT)
www.acpat.org

Frank Baines Saddlery (Reflex saddle)
Northcote Street, Walsall, England
www.frankbaines-saddlery.com

Peggy Cummings, Connected Riding
www.connectedriding.com

HorseSense Saddlery (for Elevator Bridle)
Solihull Riding Club,
Four Ashes Road
Bentley Heath, Solihull
England B93 8QE
www.elevator.gg

Joyce Harman DVM, MRCVS
www.harmanyequine.com

Kangaroo Bits
Bridgeman Street
Walsall, England WS2 9LS
www.kangaroobits.com

McTimoney Chiropractic Association
3 Oxford Court, St James Road
Brackley, Northamptonshire
England NN13 7XY
www.mctimoney-chiropractic.org

Photonic Torch Therapy
www.galesphotonictherapy.com

Probalance Probiotic Equine
Marketing Ltd
Aberbanc, Llandysul
Ceredigion, Wales SA44 5NP
www.probalanceuk.com

Amy Snow and Nancy Zidonis
Tallgrass Animal Acupressure
4559 Red Rock Drive
Larkspur, USA, CO 80118
www.animalacupressure.com

Nick Thompson BSc (Hons), BVMBS,
VetMFHom, MRCVS, Holisticvet Ltd,
Weston Chiropractic Clinic
Apthorp, Weston Road
Bath, England BA1 2XT
www.holisticvet.co.uk

Further Reading

Connected Groundwork Peggy Cummings
(ISBN 09-75921703)
Connected Riding Peggy Cummings and
Diana Deterding (ISBN 09-61131497)
A Bit of Magic Alixe Etherington
The Horse's Pain Free and Saddle Fit
Book Joyce Harman DVM, MRCVS (ISBN
1-872119-80-8)
The Chosen Road KC LaPierre (ISBN 0-
9748585-0-1)
The Horse in Motion Sarah Pilner,
Samantha Elmhurst and Zoe Davies
(ISBN0-632-05137-X)
Understand your Icelandic Horse Rikke
Mark Schultz (ISBN 87-98918-3-1)
Getting in TTouch Linda Tellington Jones
with Sybil Taylor (ISBN 1-872119-09-3)
Improve your Horse's Wellbeing Linda
Tellington Jones (ISBN 1-872119-18-2)
A Whole Bit Better Dale, Ron and Bob
Myler
Equine Acupressure – a working manual
Nancy Zidonis (ISBN 0-964-59823-X)

ACKNOWLEDGEMENTS

Thanks to Peggy Cummings, Joyce Harman DVM MRCVS, Robyn Hood, HorseWorld, Lucinda Stockley and Equine Dentistry Australia, Tallgrass Publishing, Nick Thompson BSc (Hons), BVMBS, VetMFHom, MRCVS. Also thanks to all those who help with the horses at Tilley Farm: Lorna Brown, Tina Constance, Mags Denness, Shelley Hawkins, Tully Knight, Eleanor Pearce and Sarah Sims, and to Jo Weeks, my editor.

Index